children born of wildfire

Praise for *Children Born of Wildfire*

"*Children Born of Wildfire* is a tragic, moving, occasionally amusing, and absolutely compelling story. Perfectly striking that incredibly difficult balance between presenting a life few of us can truly imagine, with enough humor to allow the reader a breath or two, Angela keeps you dying to find out what came next. Bravely revealing the darkness of growing up in a dysfunctional and abusive family, *Children Born of Wildfire* takes you on an intense emotional journey, ultimately demonstrating the amazing strength of two sisters who, against all odds, found a path to normality and happiness."

Nicholas Harvey, *USA Today* bestselling mystery and thriller author

"This memoir will be a healing help to many who have experienced the unsettling of belonging, the betrayal of abuse, and the disease of untreated mental illness within families."

Brian Dolleman, author of *An Invitation to Peace & Rest*

"*Children Born of Wildfire* is an epic tale that dives into a dark world of childhood betrayal and abuse, and emerges onto the path of healing through resilience, love, forgiveness and faith. A remarkable journey."

Victress Hitchcock, author of *A Tree with My Name on It* and *Who Knew? 23 Poems on Aging*

"I have heard countless childhood stories across my years working in chaplaincy and pastoral care. At times, the tales people tell of their early years are proverbial 'rainbows and lollipops' stories, and to be honest, I tend to question their validity. I have learnt that no one has a perfect upbringing, and there are life stories I've heard over the years that have been unbelievably traumatic.

Very rarely do people recall, reconcile, and skillfully retell their past with any kind of heartfelt coherence. Why? Because integrating our losses and pain is a lifelong soul-crafting undertaking. Thankfully, there is a growing body of survivors, like Angela Hoy, author of *Children Born of Wildfire*, who are penning their memoirs and sharing hope for healing."

David Tensen, author of *The Wrestle*, *Winters Never Last*, and *The Kid Without a Costume*

"Angela Hoy masterfully weaves a heartbreaking yet hopeful journey of healing and redemption through the power of love and connection."
Rochelle Finzel, author of Run of My Life

"Hoy gives voice not just to her own singular past, but to the experiences of countless others who are still finding the courage to speak. *Children Born of Wildfire* is brave, beautifully written, and profoundly moving."
Ger Killeen, author of Signs Following and
A Stone That Will Leap Over the Waves

"After reading Angela Hoy's riveting new book *Children Born of Wildfire*, I wanted to immediately reach out and hug her. Learning firsthand how an innocent little girl could be so thoughtlessly treated by her mother and the string of men in her mom's life. Guilty, too, were her grandparents. Yet, she showed the magnificent resilience of the human spirit. Not once did reading such a heavy topic make me want to turn away. Indeed, I could not stop reading it because I knew she would eventually win. And win she has. What a powerful message for others being mistreated. For a first-time author, the nuance and the descriptive phrases made me gasp out loud. You, too, will applaud Angela for this book and for her triumph in overcoming all that stood in her way."
Jeff Burnside, investigative journalist and author of
Cashup Davis: The Inspiring Life of a Secret Mentor

"I was glad to have had the opportunity to read an advance copy of Angela Hoy's heartbreakingly honest debut memoir, *Children Born of Wildfire*. Angela describes how she (age 4) and her younger sister Janie (age 2) were abducted from their home and their loving father by their maternal grandparents. After the kidnapping they had a chaotic childhood, experiencing much physical, emotional, verbal, and sexual abuse. But as adults, healing came through a remarkable turn of events. This is, ultimately, a hopeful story of resilience and the power of forgiveness."
Diane Papalia Zappa, author of The Married Widow
and Dear Bobby: My Grief Journey

children born of wildfire

a memoir

Angela Hoy

BOLD STORY PRESS

CHEVY CHASE, MARYLAND

Bold Story Press
Chevy Chase, MD 20815
www.boldstorypress.com

Copyright © 2025 by Angela Hoy. The stories in this book are true to the best of my recollection. However, names have been changed throughout to protect the privacy of living individuals.

All rights reserved. No part of this book may be reproduced or used in any manner without written permission of the copyright owner except for the use of quotations in a book review. Requests for permission or further information should be submitted through info@boldstorypress.com.

First edition: May 2025
Library of Congress Control Number: 2024926527
ISBN: 978-1-954805-70-5 (paperback)
ISBN: 978-1-954805-71-2 (e-book)

Cover and interior design by KP Books
Printed in the United States of America
10 9 8 7 6 5 4 3 2 1

For my father and my sister,
who loved me from the beginning.
And for everyone who has survived
the trauma of childhood abuse:

What happened to you was not your fault.
You are not forgotten, and you are loved.
You deserve a good and peaceful life.

preface

Whenever I took a poetry or prose class, fragments of my childhood experiences kept appearing in my writing. Multiple times I found myself writing about a vivid memory of an event that happened on a beach when I was four and about several quirky scenes with my grandmother. The stories wanted to be told, and I decided to use these and other recurring memories as a starting point for this book. Initially, I wrote the recollections to be funny; but when I eventually came to terms with the entirety of my young life, I allowed the undercurrents of fear and sadness to flow into the narration.

As is common among survivors of adverse childhood experiences, I'd compartmentalized memories as a means of self-protection, putting each trauma in a separate mental box. I rarely reflected on more than one or two at a time. Releasing and connecting the contents of all of the boxes into a complete life story was distressing.

In the same way, descriptions in this book of abuse suffered by my sister and I, particularly as children, could be hard to read. There are accounts of emotional, physical, and sexual abuse of children that precede the redemptive ending. Most of those memories are, sadly, still distinct in our minds, as is much of the verbal abuse. Where I haven't been able to remember specifics of conversations, I've reconstructed them in the spirit of that time, using words common to the speaker. I frequently consulted with my sister to get her memory of events and spoke often to my father and other family members about their experiences and recollections.

Children continue to be abused and neglected by their own families; such cruelty and violence is abhorrent but remains the ongoing reality for too many young lives. Misplaced shame and blame have kept much of this history out of the public eye. My response is to provide an honest recounting of the trauma my sister and I suffered and its impact so that people will understand what survivors are trying to overcome. Abusers and their enablers should be in the spotlight.

Resentment tells me that the abuse should never have happened. But it did, and I've arrived at a place of acceptance about my history. That acceptance has led to an overall peace in my life—something that gradually emerged in my thirties and forties after I faced the pain and understood and used the process of forgiveness. Today, I live with my many shortcomings, laugh as often as possible, and lean on my evolving faith.

I've included a few poems in my memoir, including three of mine—"Time Travel," "The Quest," and "Family Tree"—hoping they will speak to survivors who may be grappling with unspoken emotions. In my writer's mind, poetry is a way of distilling and conveying feelings and experiences the poet—and often the reader—can't articulate any other way. Those feelings need an outlet.

As I wrote this story, I went back into counseling, which was a gift. I've also discovered physical therapy for my long-suffering vagus nerve. I've slowly accepted that I will have to keep adjusting how I carry my past, that I will need to forgive again when I react to a triggering experience, that the frightened little girl will sometimes appear and need reassurance, and that gratitude is a protecting anchor.

With this book, the breath I held during all of my childhood has been fully released.

contents

Preface vii

part one 1
 CHAPTER 1 Swallowed 3
 CHAPTER 2 The Magic Kingdom 7
 CHAPTER 3 Breathless 17
 CHAPTER 4 Vanished 21
 CHAPTER 5 A Refuge 29
 CHAPTER 6 Courage 33
 CHAPTER 7 Ice and Shadows 37
 CHAPTER 8 The Little Cottage 43
 CHAPTER 9 The Trading Post 49
 CHAPTER 10 Angels 53
 CHAPTER 11 Embroidery 55
 CHAPTER 12 All the Right Doors 59
 CHAPTER 13 The News According to Grandma 65
 CHAPTER 14 Shane and Pinky 71
 CHAPTER 15 Waiting for Mary 75
 CHAPTER 16 My Special Ladies 79
 CHAPTER 17 A Rescue Mission 83
 CHAPTER 18 Silver Bells 89
 CHAPTER 19 Tiny Lions 91
 CHAPTER 20 Departure 93

CHAPTER 21 Off to the Suburbs 99
CHAPTER 22 Tentacles 105
CHAPTER 23 Underwater 109
CHAPTER 24 Flower Doctors 113
CHAPTER 25 Lithium Dream 117
CHAPTER 26 The Family Ghost 121

part two 129
CHAPTER 27 Phone Calls and Pixie Cuts 131
CHAPTER 28 Butterflies and Beer 135
CHAPTER 29 The Cost of Pizza 139
CHAPTER 30 Drama Queen 143
CHAPTER 31 The Separation 147
CHAPTER 32 Paradise 153
CHAPTER 33 True North 159
CHAPTER 34 The Descent 165
CHAPTER 35 Farm Animals 173
CHAPTER 36 Survivors 181
CHAPTER 37 Lost and Found 187
CHAPTER 38 Cherubs 191
CHAPTER 39 Reunion 195
CHAPTER 40 Near Misses 201

part three 205
CHAPTER 41 Grandma's Funeral 207
CHAPTER 42 Grandpa's Broken Heart 211
CHAPTER 43 You Can't Argue with Cancer 215
CHAPTER 44 A Bitter Tapestry 221
CHAPTER 45 Fire Follower 229
CHAPTER 46 Ashes 231
CHAPTER 47 Disappointments 235
CHAPTER 48 Dental Requiem 241

CHAPTER 49 The Nightmare Speaks   245
CHAPTER 50 Unrequited Love   249
CHAPTER 51 Growing Roots   253
CHAPTER 52 Redemption   259

Afterword   265
Acknowledgments   271
Endnotes   273
About the Author   275
About Bold Story Press   277

 part one

CHAPTER 1

swallowed

I don't remember when I began having nightmares, but they started early. One nightmare in particular recurred for years, always the same, always with my little sister Janie and me as small children, perhaps when we were five and three, at its center.

In my dream, I walk down a long, spiraling stairway with my sister beside me. We hold hands; we are lost. Everything around us is stone, like a castle—the stairs, the walls, even the high ceiling. There are a few window openings far above our heads; through them I can see blue sky and puffy clouds. I look to see if I can recognize anything around us, but nothing is familiar to me except my sister. We reluctantly and nervously continue down the stairs. My breaths are short and anxious. As I touch the wall to steady myself, the stone chills my fingers.

The stairway is not well lit; about ten or so steps ahead of us it is pitch dark. I turn to look back and see a room at the top of the stairs, and I want to go back up because it is brightly lit. But something pulls me back down toward the dark, slowly and deliberately forcing me to take another step, and another, and another, stair after stair. I don't want to—I don't like the dark. The staircase goes on forever; it seems unending. I look back up at the windows, hoping someone will appear and help us, but there is only sky.

Then, somehow, Janie is no longer beside me. I look around, panicked, and see her several steps below me, out of my reach. In my dream I might have called out, "Janie, wait, wait, no, no!" or I might have lost my voice to fear. I no longer remember all the details of the dream. In my heart I know she is in terrible danger.

Suddenly a menacing male voice calls out from the depths below. It is both laughing and threatening. I am so afraid. The sound reverberates through my body, flows over and around me. I feel as though I am being swallowed whole. When the voice speaks, the stairway flashes brightly for a second like lightning, illuminating our terror, and then we are in complete and suffocating darkness for a moment until the dim light returns. The windows have disappeared. No one is coming to help.

Janie begins to cry, and while she is being pulled farther down the stairs, she manages to twist enough to reach back one hand. She weeps and cries out using my childhood nickname, "Gee, Gee, help me!" I see her little blonde head, and I lean forward but realize I cannot move. I am no longer being pulled down, but I am stuck. The terrible voice and its laughing boomed deeper and closer. I somehow know it is coming up the stairs.

At this point in my nightmare, I always woke up gasping and could not go back to sleep unless the light was on. As a youngster, I could not have known that this dream represented not only my immediate fears but my apprehension about those to come.

Throughout our growing-up years, family members and other inappropriate guardians made monumental mistakes and did appalling things, leaving two vulnerable girls at the swirling center without an escape hatch.

CHAPTER 2

the magic kingdom

I n the late 1950s when parents split up, typically the children went with the mother. My sister and I were an exception to that practice. Over time, I was able to gather bits and pieces of information from our grandmother, and after we were reunited with our father, he filled in the blanks about how he met our mother and moved from England to Canada and why we did not go with our mother when our parents' marriage shattered.

Our father Albert Hoy turned eighteen in December 1946, and he was conscripted into the Royal Army Service Corps. World War II had ended in September 1945, but Britain kept its military draft going for some years beyond that date. Al's company had six weeks of training and then shipped to Germany for a two-year deployment. However, after Russia began taking control of Eastern Europe, Britain maintained its military presence in Germany for another year, believing war could again be imminent. In 1949, Al was discharged and returned to Cambridgeshire, the county northeast of London where he grew up. He was the oldest of five children and had a brother and three sisters. His quiet manner, tall frame, and curly brown hair echoed his late father, who had died when Al was ten.

When he returned home, he met Rose Stumely, a teenage member of the Women's Land Army who had been billeted at his mother's place. Known as "land girls," members of the WLA were initially volunteers, but in December of 1941 conscription of most women between ages eighteen and sixty began for "war work," including the WLA.[1] England desperately needed more workers to grow food and fill jobs formerly held by men and sent these women all over the country. Of course, young women could still volunteer, which Rose appeared to have done.

After the end of World War II, Cecil and Florence Stumely—Rose's parents and my maternal grandparents—traveled in 1948 to Egypt, where my grandfather had been posted by the Royal Air Force following his squadron service throughout the war. They took their children, Rose and her younger brother Stewart. It wasn't long before my grandmother Florence and my mother Rose made clear they did not like being in a hot, dusty, and mosquito-rich country. Rose must have found a way to get back to England at some point during the late 1940s, while Grandma and Stewart remained with Cecil as he served his full deployment. This could explain how Rose managed to be serving in the Women's Land Army while she was younger than conscription age, which her father probably would have prohibited.

The Hoy family's row home was small, and Al, his widowed mother, and four siblings filled it. But they found a corner for seventeen-year-old Rose, who had traveled from the south to fulfill her assignment. Al, now twenty-one, returned to work at the butcher shop where he'd apprenticed before the war. Rose worked on a farm about five miles from her billet and rode her bike there and back each day. It wasn't long before Al was smitten with beautiful Rose, and they began going to the "picture show" and other local places. Rose was outgoing and curvaceous with wavy brown hair and flashing green eyes. Not long after they met the WLA was disbanded. and Rose found work locally. She and Al dated for a couple of years, and by then Al was besotted, unable to believe his luck at finding such a wonderful person. Photos of them with a group of friends from around 1950 show his tall frame bending toward the camera and her glancing over at him, both with splendidly broad smiles.

In 1952 when Rose was nineteen, Cecil and Florence announced that the family, including Rose and Stewart, were moving to Canada. At that time Canada heavily promoted emigration from Britain, and many answered the call, hoping for a better life without rationing, bombed-out buildings, and a wrecked economy. Rose told Al that she was leaving, and he panicked because he didn't have the money to pay for passage on the transatlantic voyage to accompany her. She went home and declared that she wasn't going to Canada unless her sweetheart Al was included, and her father reluctantly paid for an extra ticket, enabling Al to leave his English village and join Rose to sail cross the Atlantic. Paying for Al's passage was probably my grandfather's way of getting Rose on the ship without a protracted quarrel.

On the ship Empress of Scotland, Al found himself about six decks down, while Rose and her family were located on an upper deck with orders to stay away from Al. Having served as an officer in the air force, my grandfather was accustomed to being obeyed; however, he was no match for Rose's wiles,

Rose and Albert begin their new life in Canada, 1953

and she found ways to spend time with Al. Desperately in love with Rose, Al could not imagine his life without her, but he was quickly learning that his future father-in-law disliked him with an inexplicable intensity. Al came from humble beginnings, and likely my grandfather thought Rose could and should find someone of better standing—that is, with more money, education, and status. (Although I think my conclusion is sound, it is interesting that on the 1921 Census of England and Wales, Grandpa's father is listed as a farmer.) Grandpa was never charitable toward Al and seemed to get satisfaction from growling insults at him, often while clenching one of his ever-present cigars between his teeth.

The family, plus Al, landed in Montreal, Quebec and then traveled on to Toronto, Ontario for immigration processing. With his background in meat cutting, Al was given an appointment at Loblaw's, a local grocery chain, where he was hired as a butcher and continued to work for some years. Rose got a job in a bank. They married in 1953 and eventually rented a comfortable two-story house on a gently sloping street in Oakville near Toronto. Photos of them at that time show a well-dressed, good-looking couple smiling pleasantly at the camera. My maternal grandparents bought a house in the same town. I was born in February 1955, and my sister Janie came along in February 1957.

In 1957, when I was a toddler and my sister a baby, Mum took us to England, but our father stayed behind. Mum visited

Cecil, Rose, Florence, and Al. Ontario 1954

both sides of the family and was her usual social self. All three of my father's sisters adored Janie and me. It wasn't long before they were alarmed that my mother would go off with me for hours and leave Janie behind in her large pram. They hovered over the tiny blonde baby, took care of her, and worried about her. One of my aunties wanted to confront Mum about the neglect. However, my paternal grandmother, Mabel Hoy, whom we called Nana, could not see any good coming of an intervention.

During that same 1957 trip, Mum managed to have an affair with the husband of one of our father's sisters, leading to disruption and heartbreak in that family. Astoundingly, the uncle actually followed Mum back to Canada by stowing away on a ship headed there, but no one knows what happened when he landed. A few months on, after the uncle had returned to England, one of Dad's sisters called him to break the news about the cheating and the family upheaval that followed.

My parents' marriage blew apart in 1959 when our mother left our father for a work colleague, a younger guy. I have a memory of this man running through our house blasting away on a trumpet, Mum following him and shrieking with laughter, and me—all of three years old—trailing in her wake, always up for a party. I didn't quite understand who he was, but he was a lot of fun and Mum liked him, so that was good enough for me. Mercifully, I have no memory of when our father came home months later to find them together. Mum boomeranged back to England, possibly with her lover in tow, and left us with Dad. She was twenty-seven; Dad was thirty-one. Their marriage had lasted six years.

Mum was a charmer with a sense of humor. She always could make me laugh. But underneath that wit and hilarity was a mean streak as big as a Great Lake. I was to learn that her departure from our family was tumultuous, though I remember nothing. Years afterward, longtime friends of Dad would share stories of her nasty exit that stabbed at my heart and made me fearful that I might carry her traits. Even as a young woman, her trail was littered with broken and battered spirits.

Dad had wedded a whirlwind, a typhoon, a wildfire of a woman, and after she disappeared that year, he took on the role of single parent and began rebuilding for our family of three in Oakville. I have a few scattered windows of recall back to my toddler world. In one, Dad and I are sitting on the back steps at dusk watching fireflies winking and flashing across the yard. I had never seen them before and leaned forward, gripping my knees and squinting into the darkening landscape. Seized with a desire to hold them close and watch them, I asked, "Daddy, can we get a jar so I can catch one?"

"No darling. Those are little fairies, and they don't like being in jars. Best just to watch them dance and let them be free."

Another memory has remained faithful. I began reading and counting early, so Dad taught me to play simple card games. We would sit in the sunlit living room, me bouncing up and down and clapping my hands as Dad dealt the cards for a powerful game of Snap, a matching game. "Hurry up, Daddy, let's play cards!" The player who got the most matches won. I loved the game and would slap my card down on a match, yelling "Snap, Daddy! Snap! I got one!"

He always acted amazed and would bend his six-foot-two frame down to peer at the cards and then straighten up and reply, "So you did! What a smart girl." I "won" a stunning number of games against my father and became a three-year-old card shark.

Being so young at that time, Janie doesn't have many memories, but she does remember happily sitting on Dad's knee while he gently brushed her thick blonde hair, so relieved that Mum was not at the other end of the brush. When Mum had the brush, her head always hurt and she would be scolded for any complaints or tears.

At some point during my fourth year, after Mum had left the marriage, my maternal grandparents dropped by for a visit. In his recounting of this part of his life, our father said that Grandma seemed concerned about the strain of the separation on him and talked to him earnestly about how all of the upset was affecting my sister and me. She had a proposal for him, which he received with caution because he'd already learned her grip on the truth was slippery. She and Grandpa would take us two girls on a wonderful trip to Disneyland in California! She spoke with enthusiasm. It would be such an adventure to see the new theme park. He could have a much-needed break, and the girls could see the Magic Kingdom! Just think of it!

Nope. Our father was having none of it; he'd already learned not to trust this family. But she and Grandpa came for another visit, and then again. Grandma continued to promote the benefits of a trip: The girls could have a vacation just like the grownups! Such fun! After a few visits and discussions, Dad finally relented, thinking my sister and I could experience something amazing. "Tremendous!" she probably exclaimed. "Brilliant! Absolutely *smashing*!" She would have pulled these words from her generous stock of adjectives and applied them liberally, wedging open the chink in his armor.

All she needed was $100 to help fund the trip. She got my father's permission and his money, and off we went with our little suitcases in Grandma and Grandpa's car, waving and giggling and eager. Dad didn't see who was behind the wheel that day, because only Grandma came into the house to collect us.

We did not know that we would never return to our two-story home sitting on the gentle slope in Oakville, where the fireflies winked and where I listened to thunderstorms while bouncing on a spring-loaded play horse in the glassed-in porch. And where I watched out the living room window for Dad to come home from work so I could run outside squealing, "Hello Daddy! Hello!"

My sister and I did not know that we were an Amber Alert in the making. It would be years before children were given full legal rights and before family-engineered kidnappings ended up on the wrong side of the law.

We did not know that none of the many homes after our father's home would feel safe for long. We did not know that after we waved goodbye on our happy ride to the Magic Kingdom, we would not see our father again for twenty-seven years.

CHAPTER 3

breathless

We girls rode off to begin our magical adventure, according to a carefully planned itinerary that had not been shared with Dad. Grandma didn't drive, so either Grandpa or Uncle Stewart (then 22) would have been behind the wheel. We traveled across the Canadian border and deep into the US and then curved up along the west coast, stopping at beaches along the way. Beaches were among my grandmother's favorite places, and mine as well.

One beachside park we visited turned into an unforgettable memory. Sometime during my young adult years, I asked my grandmother about that day and pieced it together with my own recollections. At the park, the noise of the Pacific Ocean and shrieks of seagulls were fantastically deafening and exciting for me. I am sure I had the wiggles after being in the car for hours, so after Grandma helped us into our bathing suits, I got loose from her hand and ran straight toward groups of people and kids playing in mounds of white sand.

The sand was warm and soft—it felt like kitten fur on my feet. I kept on running past the beachgoers and down into the water, giggling and splashing. I promptly forgot the family rule to wade only up to my knees. When I was thigh deep in the water, I turned to wave at Grandma, who had hold of my two-year-old sister, a small figure wrapped almost entirely in a towel to protect her fair skin from the sun.

Having lived all of my four short years around lakes and rivers, I welcomed water as my friend. When Grandma started jumping up and down, I thought she was excited for me, so I waved even harder and gave her my best smile. Then the wave swallowed me whole, and I was no longer visible from the shore. Churning around in its cold heart, sand and water rushed into and past my eyes, nose, and ears as I rolled and rolled. Inside the wave, it was quiet except for a strange rushing sound. Up and down were gone, and I couldn't feel my arms and legs. It was dark, then light, then dark, then light again as the water swirled and I spun. I thought the light shining through the water was pretty.

Just as I began to gasp for air, my body flew from the wave. Splat. I landed face down on the wet, hard beach. The water was gone. I was chewing grit, my eyes hurt, and my nose and ears were plugged with water and sand. My uncle, usually laughing and teasing, grabbed me up with a serious look on his face, and Grandma was screaming full tilt in her British falsetto. I remember thinking that my bathing suit was really heavy. Then I realized it was full of sand.

Reflecting on this episode in later years, my grandmother said that she was frantic to the point of hysteria. She thought I was gone, lost in the riptide and the waves to become a bloated drowning victim. She was already on edge because she had no idea where my mother was and hadn't known for months. The trail had gone cold in Europe.

For two little girls, our special trip to Disneyland in 1959 ought to have been full of special memories to last a lifetime—except that neither of us has any memories at all of the Magic Kingdom.

CHAPTER 4

vanished

Nearly sixty years later, I visited my father just a couple of months before his eighty-ninth birthday, hoping he could help me sort through my misty recollections of those very early years. Asking my mother or her family resulted in a maze of half-truths and fabrications; they'd all passed away and it was time to sort fact from fiction.

On a rainy September day in 2018, I arrived at my father's cozy townhome in a suburb of Vancouver, British Columbia. Parking in the familiar driveway, I walked past the front yard, a whimsical mix of plants, pottery, and statues arranged by Marlene, my father's wife of thirty-five years. They both puttered among the leaves and blooms when weather and health allowed. Around the side of the house, beneath a couple of massive cedar trees, their compact RV was parked, ready for adventures that came less often due to Dad's failing eyesight and more fragile health. I thought about all the days I'd pulled into his driveway during the past thirty-three years and smiled, recalling a wealth of happy times.

Dad and I settled in the serene blue-and-white living room to chat. I sat close because of his hearing aids. Marlene braved the downpour outside to go shopping, so he and I had some quiet time together, complete with cups of tea and chatter about the weather and the past week. He was uncharacteristically serious and had not made any of his usual wry jokes. We pivoted to the past, and after a few questions he got a distant look on his face and told me that he really tried to get Grandpa to see his side, his way of looking at life, but it was no use. Grandpa hurled insults every time he saw Dad, then a young man in his twenties. There was no explaining the depth of that hatred. Then I asked Dad about what happened when the Disneyland vacation was supposed to be over.

In 1959, at the agreed-upon time for our return, Dad called our grandparents' number to check when my sister and I would be dropped off at his home. Our grandfather answered the phone. He told Dad that our grandmother had taken us on an extended vacation. "In fact," he said, "You are never going to see the girls again. Ever."

Stunned, Dad's response was, "But why?"

Grandpa launched into a tirade of insults. "You are nothing but a whimpering, weak-kneed dog . . . " He spat out a flood of abusive invectives.

Probably around the time that Grandma took my sister and me into western Canada via Washington State, Dad realized that he had funded his own daughters' kidnapping. Together, my grandparents used their toolbox of lies, cunning, and denigration to separate us from our father. As I sat in Dad's living room, I was dismayed to be related to those cold and calculating people.

After this conversation, Dad told me that he was "just existing" while continuing to work. The rain drummed on the skylight as we held hands and talked about how traumatized he had been. He told me he wasn't equipped for what they had done to his little family, making off with his young girls and leaving him in a state of shock. "I had no idea how to fight them," he said softly. "I wasn't used to a family fighting."

His voice got quieter as he recounted what happened next. A short time after that awful phone call, Grandpa called again and said the children needed their beds. He said he wanted to go to the house to pick them up when Dad wouldn't be there. As we sat there in his living room, Dad briefly paused recounting the story because of the noisy rain. He turned to look at me, and I saw tears forming in the corners of his eyes. "I said it was OK for him to go into the house and get the beds. I should have been stronger," he said, "but I wasn't." He wanted his girls to have their familiar beds.

When Dad got home from work on the day Grandpa picked up the beds, the entire house had been emptied. Grandpa had brought a moving van and cleared out every single thing except for one bed and one table. Dad realized that he'd been tricked yet again, and then he learned that my grandparents had left Oakville. He didn't know where they were going, but they had his two girls and they were gone.

As my father recounted the story, the pouring rain matched the tears that again broke through and flowed down his face. "Angela, I am really, really sorry, but I didn't have the courage to go to the house when your grandfather was there and face him." His voice grew reedy, and he stared into the rain, beyond the decades, back to that horrendous day. "I just couldn't go and face him. I hated him for what he'd done. I felt betrayed, I felt whipped, I felt like a little dog."

I listened to the sound of rain drumming on the skylight, too stunned to speak. Years of work to forgive and understand my mother and her family raced through my mind as I patted Dad's hand. Until that fall day, I'd never known the details of how my mother's family had orchestrated kidnapping us from our father. That part of our young lives had always been described by Mum as a "holiday with Grandma and Grandpa." I couldn't believe the deliberateness, the cruelty, and the audacity of it all. But my mind recalibrated; I *could* believe it because I, too, had lived it. I ached deeply, beyond tears, beyond rational thought, beyond peace, and I felt once again the spreading darkness of my childhood that stretched over my young adult years. I was frustrated and disturbed because Grandma, Grandpa, and Mum were all dead, and yet they were still hurting us.

After my father apologized again, I said, "Dad, if you had gone to the house that day when Grandpa was emptying it, he might have killed you. He had an awful temper. You had a guardian angel with you that day. And I think your life had a greater purpose."

Dad turned to look at me, his face still lined with pain, sadness, and regret. "My life has a greater purpose *now*."

The rain slowed to a patter as Dad took a deep breath and continued his account. After his house on the gentle slope in Oakville had been emptied, he moved to a basement room in town and kept existing. He went to see a lawyer and paid him $100—a significant sum in the early 1960s—to find us and arrange for visiting rights. The lawyer used a private investigator and eventually told Dad, "You are never going to get the children back, no matter how hard you try." When Dad asked why, the lawyer replied, "Those people are evil." Weeks went by. The lawyer produced paperwork indicating that our mother was back in the picture. The address was blacked out. At that point, my father was further wounded. The lawyer asked him, "Have you ever abused those children?"

Dad responded, "No, of course I haven't."

The lawyer replied, "Two women have sworn to a judge that you abused the children."

Dad said he cried out, "Oh my God, what is going to happen?"

He was determined to keep trying to find us, and even though his lawyer advised him against going to court, he took legal action. At the courthouse, Dad stated to the judge, "I'm not lying to you. I have never touched those children in any improper way." He insisted that he loved his girls and would never hurt them.

The judge looked at Dad and said, "I'm inclined to believe you, but these are two little girls. They need to be in a family." The judge went on to say that he was not going to grant Dad visiting rights.

Dad responded incredulously, "I can't see them at all?" The decision had already been made—likely before Dad even got to the courtroom.

After he recounted this, we sat quietly together, pulling ourselves back to the present. A wind got up outside, and I glanced at the cedar trees in the backyard as they splattered rainwater and needles onto the patio. Dad's voice cracked as he said to me, "I loved you children . . . I loved you something terrible . . . I never abused you . . . " his voice faded while more tears dripped from his vivid blue eyes. I tried to reassure him, patting his hand again, and said, "I have only the best memories of you, Dad."

Dad continued to look for us. Mum got a court order to garnish his wages for child support, which he paid for years out of his salary as a meat cutter without ever knowing where we were. He told me that when he first started paying support, after his modest living expenses were covered, he had $5 left over each month.

Concerned about my aged father reliving these painful memories, I stopped asking him questions. But as the rain and the trees continued their autumn tango, he had something more to share about the destruction of his marriage.

"When your mother left us and went to England, she told your grandfather that 'she didn't want anything to do with you kids.' She told him that he could have you. She didn't even want you. She didn't even want you *beautiful* children. But your grandfather told her that she was going to '*get those children* and she was going to *look after them*.'" Even as Mum was in the process of leaving the marriage, it appears Grandpa was already plotting to get us girls away from our father and try to force her to care for us.

I did not ask Dad how he knew this, wanting to avoid another recounting of a painful scene about Mum leaving him. I knew the words sounded exactly like something Grandpa would say. He was always a stickler for obligations, responsibilities and being sensible—at least when he was trying to control Mum.

I redirected the conversation and spoke about the happy thirty-plus years that he, Janie, and I have all had together since we had been reunited in 1986. I said, "We have redeemed all the lost time; we are a loving family. We are not living in a web of lies." Finally, we ran out of words and held hands quietly, exhausted, listening to the patter of the rain.

On my way home, I pondered why my grandparents went to diabolical lengths to separate us girls from our father. My guess is that there was a series of untruths and exaggerations concocted by our mother, who learned her craft of slight-to-great fabrications at the feet of her mother. To absolve herself of any accountability and to divert attention from her own shabby behavior, Mum must have told her parents what the British would call "a pack of lies."

Those fictional creations were grafted into an existing formula of family dislike and disapproval of our father, creating a critical mass that resulted in us being swept away from him. A conveniently large dose of denial helped my grandparents ignore the impudent truth that their daughter had committed adultery—in her own home.

It is unrealistic to believe that my mother's headstrong and self-centered behavior suddenly appeared after she got married. She had at least two affairs during her short marriage to Dad. She was young, intent on amusing herself, self-centered, and irresponsible. She did not want to be tied down with children. Still, it appears her parents strongly believed that we kids belonged in their branch of the family and saw the three of us—me, Janie, and Mum—as an inseparable unit. This set of beliefs allowed them to either ignore or explain away the reality that their daughter was incapable of being even an adequate mother.

Very likely, my grandparents also wanted to help my mother salvage her life in order to protect their own reputations. This pattern of my grandparents shoring up my mother's failings would be repeated throughout our childhood.

CHAPTER 5

a refuge

On that rainy-day visit to Dad's house, my father also talked about his life after we had been taken. Heartbroken, he told his friend and work colleague Ben that he could not believe what had happened. Ben wasted no time bringing my father home to meet his wife Jean and their kids. At the time, the couple had three small children, and they drew Dad into their family. He became a regular every Sunday afternoon and played with their kids, then enjoyed some rounds of poker with the grownups.

Dad gave me Ben and Jean's number, and a few days on, I called them. Now in their eighties and in poor health, I asked what they remember about that time and invited them to reflect on their friendship with my father. Ben responded to my specific questions about the time immediately after the abduction with "it was a sad time, a very sad time," either reluctant to say much or unable to remember. He does recall my father sitting in their Toronto-area home, weeping. Jean got on the phone and said Dad's sorrow over our absence had been profound.

As I listened to Jean, I recalled meeting her when I was thirty-two, not long after our marvelous reunion with Dad. Jean was a spitfire in the best sense of the term, big-hearted, plain-spoken, and loyal to her friends. At one point when the two of us were alone in the kitchen, she recounted something my father had told her. When the marriage was breaking up and Mum had made it clear she was leaving, Dad fell on the floor in shock and begged her not to leave him. She looked at him in disgust and kicked him, calling him names, before walking over him and out of the room.

On the phone, our conversation continued. Jean recalled that back then, none of them had much money, and they found ways to enjoy life close to home. Jean felt the time that Al spent with them and their kids was a comfort to him, and Ben reflected that it was a distraction from the pain of losing his two daughters. What they really wanted to talk about is how much they enjoyed their special friend. They recounted at length how they would scrape together enough money to go on shared vacations and how they kept that tradition going through the decades and around the world until ill health stopped them. They could not stop chatting about all the happy memories that populated their much-cherished friendship.

Ben remembered inviting himself to the honeymoon when Dad married Marlene in 1983. Marlene had planned a romantic cruise for two. In the end, nearly a dozen friends booked passage on the same sailing to celebrate. Now in the twilight of his life, Ben laughed heartily as he reflected on how much fun it was. Later I asked Marlene about this unusual celebration. She told me that at first she was nonplussed to learn that a crowd of Dad's friends had invited themselves along for her first—and only—honeymoon.

Then she told herself, "Hey, anybody can have an ordinary honeymoon!"

Jean, Ben, and I wrapped up our call. "Your dad was always patient and kind and up for some fun," Jean said, adding that he has remained that way throughout his life. Perhaps feeling that she needed to offer a contrasting truth, Jean remarked, "Angela, your mother was not a nice person." It was a remarkably tactful understatement.

CHAPTER 6

courage

Following my visit with my father and after that call with Ben and Jean, more of my memories emerged, and they resulted in a feeling of nausea that kept coming back for days.

It was mostly due to a feeling of guilt—the same emotion that had felled Dad for days with wave after wave of anxiety before we talked on that wet September day. It was about my sister Janie.

As a youngster, Janie was a sweet girl with her father's bright blue eyes surrounded by a mist of silver blonde hair. She was as shy and quiet as I was outgoing and cheerfully chatty. She was slender, a tiny twig; I was dark-haired and more solidly built. Janie lacked my digestive strength and had trouble with some foods. She often did not clean her plate, which for some reason was tantamount to family treason in Mum's eyes. I had already learned not to ask questions about Mum's rules.

An early memory from the shadows of my mind strengthened as I suddenly recalled how the scene had plagued me through my childhood and early adult years. Janie and I were at the kitchen table in Oakville, Ontario, and Mum was feeding Janie, who was about a year old, and I was about three. The sun was trickling through the window, and I wanted to go and play, so I had cleaned my plate and was fidgeting in my chair.

It's vague, but I remember Mum insisting that Janie keep eating and at some point, my baby sister threw up on her plate. Then the kitchen table came into sharp focus.

Our mother grabbed Janie by the front of her dress, hauled her up out of her highchair and shook her like a rag doll, screaming something like, "You better stop this! I've had enough of you, dammit!" My sister's head snapped back and forth as she sobbed and tried to breathe.

I was rooted in my chair. Somehow, I knew I should intervene but I was overcome by fear. I wanted to stop my mother. It was not right. It was horrible. I wanted to close my eyes and pretend it was not happening. I could not stop it.

Janie survived, but when we were older my sister developed a habit of sometimes slipping me food from her plate that she didn't like. I was always happy to make it disappear. I ate pretty much everything on my plate at every meal. Perhaps I consumed her portions as a kind of penance for not being able to protect her.

When I asked her in 2018, my sister did not remember the kitchen trauma. I was relieved. But she remembered another incident that I did not.

For a short time, when I was eight and Janie six, Mum enrolled us in private school. She always wanted us to have a good education with small classes and a strong curriculum. Appearances were important to her, and she liked the uniforms at our all-girls school. I was happy to be at this school.

The buildings were old and creaky and interesting, the classes were half the size of public school classes, teachers gave me lots of attention, and the grounds had trees, slopes, moss, paths, and plenty of places to explore.

One day at recess I found Janie crying in the school yard. She showed me her bruised and scraped knuckles, saying through her tears, "My fingers hurt!" At that time, many teachers used rulers and yardsticks to maintain control in classrooms. That day my sister's sin was daydreaming—she had been looking out the window instead of paying attention to the lesson.

I'm not sure how Janie's teacher conducted this particular cruelty, but usually teachers would come up from behind the student and clock their knuckles with the ruler. Hard. Sometimes they would summon a student to the front of the room, make them hold out their hands, and whack each hand once or more—hard. Some teachers would hit a student again if tears appeared. Either way, Janie's teacher must have hit her on the knuckles with the metal edge of the ruler.

Apparently, after my sister told me what had happened, I marched up to the teacher, who was supervising in the school yard, pointed a finger directly at her and bellowed, "You are a *horrible person!*" It is possible I am unable to recall this scene because there surely would have been repercussions, which are fortunately lost to me.

In reflecting on the traumatic memory of Mum abusing Janie, I have tried to understand why I did not react to help myself overcome the guilt of not rescuing her. Obviously, at this time I was young and small and probably at great risk of being knocked down myself if I had tried to stop my mother. But the freezing-in-place became my default response whenever Mum came after me or Janie in the years ahead. She literally scared me almost to death. I've read that people can become so afraid that they freeze in place, disabling their ability to respond to a frightening situation. People joke around about someone being a deer in the headlights, but for me it was real. I believe that I responded differently to the teacher because I simply was not as afraid of her as I was of my mother.

CHAPTER 7

ice and shadows

At about the same time that my father began pulling himself out of despair, our abduction-vacation had ended somewhere in southern British Columbia. From there, Grandma took my sister and me to Dawson Creek in remote northeast British Columbia, about 2,500 miles from where my father was living in Oakville, Ontario.[1] As with most of our childhood moves, I remember nothing of the relocation, but I assume a few months had transpired since we'd been taken from Dad.

At that time, Dawson Creek was a small northern town of about 10,000 people, and the main street was a dirt road that was dusty in the summer, muddy in the spring and fall, and frozen in the winter. When we arrived, Grandpa was already there, having traveled from Ontario with the family's belongings as well as the furniture he had stolen from our father. He had found and furnished a house and was working as a catering manager for the Peace River Dam project north of the city. When I turned five I started kindergarten.

Our two-story wood house was basic and not well insulated. During the long winter, I liked to chip off the ice on the inside of the upstairs windows to see how fast it would regrow. The literal chill extended to the figurative cold of my grandparents, whose regular squabbles would arc from a quiet disagreement to Grandma's voice rising thinly and Grandpa yelling "shut *up*, stupid woman, with your damn nagging!" Then Grandma would either turn and dab her eyes with her apron or leave the room, or Grandpa would bang out the front door and stomp through the never-ending snow.

One day Mum suddenly appeared at our house in Dawson Creek. By then I had become accustomed to unexplained and dramatic changes, so I took her arrival in stride and was thrilled to see her, no questions asked. Years later, Grandma told me that once she got Janie and me settled in Dawson Creek, her singular mission was to get Mum to return to Canada. Somehow, Grandma had tracked down Mum, who was either in Europe or England, and began sending letters. Then she fired off a telegram.

> WE HAVE YOUR CHILDREN STOP YOU MUST RETURN HOME AT ONCE STOP FATHER WILL PAY FOR THE TRIP STOP YOUR CHILDREN NEED YOU STOP MOTHER

I'm guessing that Mum was willing to be convinced because she'd either run out of money or got into trouble or both, and she needed a fast getaway. Once Mum had returned, this seemed like the most probable time that she and Grandma had likely decided to accuse Dad of abuse to ensure that he would never have access to us. Lying under oath was not an impediment for either of these women, if in fact they were the two women referenced by Dad's lawyer in the custody case for us girls. Making the false accusation of child abuse likely helped Mum get Dad's salary garnished for child support with no further questions or clarification needed and also cemented Grandpa's boiling hatred of Dad.

I have wondered why Mum would have created a situation that ensured she would always be responsible for children she really didn't want. Maybe she wanted to be completely rid of Dad without complications, because he knew the truth about her neglect of Janie, about her adultery with his English brother-in-law and more adultery at the end of their marriage. Possibly it was simply another way to hurt him and to ruin his reputation. Perhaps she was bowing to pressure from her parents. I imagine it was a combination of these and other reasons.

In Dawson Creek, we settled into our version of family life. Mum got a job at a local bank, Grandpa worked at the dam project, I transitioned to grade one at age six, and Grandma kept the home fires lit and cared for Janie. Grandma and Grandpa's arguments were a pale version of Mum's fights with Grandpa. Father and daughter would yell and scream without reservation. Janie and I would retreat upstairs and cling to each other or play quiet games, anything to avoid being collateral damage in the raging emotions downstairs. Often after a bad fight, Mum would have violent migraines resulting in her crying and moaning and vomiting; these episodes were so frightening to me that I thought she was dying. As time went on, I figured out that most of those fights were either about money, Mum's responsibilities to us, or her choice of friends.

In contrast, my earliest memories of my father are of his kindness, patience, and readiness to play. He was quiet and calm, and I was happy in the glow of his love. Though Janie was very young when we were abducted, she recalls feeling warmly about him. We would not be close to another kind man for many years.

In Dawson Creek, Mum's companion was Kurt. He was several years younger than her with dark hair and an unstable temperament. He had emigrated from Germany with his parents probably after World War II, and they had thick accents, which fascinated me when we visited them. Kurt's parents did not appear to like Janie and me; we remember visiting

Angela and Janie in Dawson Creek, circa 1960

them with Mum and being told to go outside and play—in the snow. Kurt's mother was stocky; she kept her hair in a severe bun and wore thick stockings that she rolled down to her knees. I'd never seen anyone who looked like her and could not keep from staring.

Grandma despised them and all Germans because of the Blitz bombings during World War II.[2] Many English cities were targeted, and with Grandpa in the Royal Air Force, she was left to protect her two children (our mother and uncle), running with them to air-raid shelters when the sirens blared. She also despised Italians and people of Japanese descent because those two countries had also been at war against England.[3] "The war, dahling. It was a *terrible* time, and those *people* were dreadful, despicable, *scum of the earth.*" I suppose it may have pleased Mum to find a boyfriend who greatly aggravated her mother.

A move from Dawson Creek to Victoria brought another shade of darkness into our young lives.

CHAPTER 8

the little cottage

We had all been living in Dawson Creek, where I attended grade one and part of grade two. Then suddenly we moved to a different city, but my memory retained nothing of this transition.

Early in 1962, Mum and Kurt packed up and took Janie and me—likely after another epic fight with Grandpa—nearly 800 miles south to Victoria, BC.[1] By this time, Mum was thirty but looked younger; Kurt was twenty-two. Either before or after that move, Grandma bought a house in Victoria and moved in, alone. Grandpa would show up once in a while for a visit, but they lived separately from that point.

At seven, I transferred to Willows Elementary in Victoria to complete grade two, which was a much larger school and a bit scary for me. I spent as much time outdoors as I possibly could because Victoria was amazing to me. It was warmer than the north; it was green and hilly and surrounded by ocean on three sides. There were creeks and rivers and parks galore. The sun shone in the summer, and there were so many more birds and not nearly so many biting bugs as in the north. It seemed like paradise after Dawson Creek.

We lived in three places that I can recall while Mum was with Kurt. The first was an apartment, and the second was a cottage at the edge of a forested area. The land surrounding our cottage was my favorite outdoor place; there was a Garry Oak grove next to it, filled with birds whistling and chirping and calling in the trees. On the ground, I could hear rustling—it sounded so alive! There were wildflowers, bushes, and rocks covered with silky-soft moss where I would sometimes startle a garter snake basking in the sun. I found endless spots to clamber around and play.

Inside the cottage, things were different. One day everyone was happy and kidding around and laughing. Mum would sing her way around the kitchen to her favorite tune on the radio while Kurt would smile from his chair. My sister and I would hold hands with her and spin in a circle, laughing and giggling in the glow of her dazzling smile.

Another day, Kurt could become wildly emotional, and Mum would pull him into their bedroom; I didn't understand, but I could still hear them. Standing in the small living room, I'd be partly riveted and partly terrified by the sounds coming through the wall, and my legs felt weak, as if my worries had fallen into them. At times, to my child's mind, his frenzied voice almost sounded like he was laughing. "Ah-*huh*, ah-*huh*, ah huh, huh, huh!" His muffled voice, frantic crying, and strange sounds would give way to Mum's voice trying to calm him down. I was surprised she didn't hit him, because that was always her solution when I had a tantrum.

While we lived in that cottage, we were regularly beaten, now by both Mum and Kurt. Her weapons of choice were wooden spoons and large hairbrushes, while my sister remembers Kurt favoring a long-handled bathroom brush. All these devices were used on our bare hands, the backs of our legs, or our rear ends. One afternoon, Kurt suddenly grabbed my arm and hit my legs and my rear end with the bristle side of a big hairbrush. At first, I laughed, thinking he was kidding, but then he hit me harder. I tried to twist away but he yanked me back, his dark eyes squinting.

I was so shocked and cried out to him, "But why are you hitting me?"

"Just because," he replied with a smile.

While we lived in that cottage there were a lot of rules that made no sense, but breaking those rules resulted in punishments. Janie remembers not being allowed to go outside for days. One day, she saw the next-door neighbor outside with her baby in a carriage, and she sneaked out to get a peek. She adored babies and always wanted to hold and cuddle them. Janie does not have many memories from that time in our lives, but this one remains clear for her, and she shared it with me. My memory of this event is fragmentary. This is what Janie told me:

> When I was looking at the baby outside, I heard Kurt come home. I tried to get back in the house before he found me, but I was not fast enough. It was wintertime, and I was wearing a blue wool coat with a cream beret, black shoes, a blue pleated skirt, and a white blouse. Kurt marched me into the kitchen—the warmest room in the house—and made me stand with my hands up in the air for what seemed like hours, wearing all those clothes. Every time I began to drop my arms, he would hit me with

a long-handled pink bathroom brush and say, "You are a bad girl!" For many years, I could not have any long-handled brushes in the bathroom because seeing them brought back that memory.

Though my own patch of memory is faint, I recall being in the living room, a wood-paneled room that always felt dark. Closing my eyes today, I can see myself standing in the middle of the living room, watching my little sister in the next room in her blue coat struggling to keep her arms up and her fair head downcast. I'd gone into the kitchen once during Janie's punishment, and Kurt hit Janie and told me if I came back, he'd keep hitting her. He wanted to keep us apart. I kept out of Kurt's sight, but I could see her struggling, quiet, suffering. I knew he was sitting there with the brush, watching her. I was rubbing one arm with the other anxiously, unconsciously. I heard his voice commanding her to "stand up straight!" My breath was choppy as I watched my sister being tortured, once again unable to help save her. It was a long and excruciating punishment for a slender five-year-old girl who loved babies.

This recollection has been among the most difficult for me to write about, even more than five decades along. I want to put my head on my desk and weep for these two little ones. My questions flow in an unanswerable circle. Where was our mother? She always made sure we looked good, our ensembles color coordinated and our hair done; did she dress Janie that day? My hair was done, too, in braids. Was she in bed with one of her constant migraines? If Mum was home, would she have allowed this? I don't want to know.

Sorrow still colors the edges of my memory. How was it that neither of the adults in our household could see us as the cute kids we were? They didn't recognize my curiosity, my readiness to study and explore. They couldn't see Janie's natural gifts of nurturing and kindness.

It is clear to me now that Kurt suffered from debilitating panic attacks and anxiety. Mum had crippling migraines and profound mood swings. Possibly they both had PTSD from World War II or may have been on the bipolar spectrum. They both had lived through the war as children in the two countries at the center of that great conflict. Their parents found a way to survive the fear and devastation that consumed Europe. Who knows what they went through? It could not have been good.

However, that doesn't excuse their repugnant behavior toward us children. Mum and Kurt's choices as adults were toxic and irresponsible and put us girls at constant risk. Furthermore, nothing Kurt went through as a child could justify his sadistic enjoyment in tormenting and harming two little girls. Nothing at all.

CHAPTER 9

the trading post

The third and possibly last house we lived in with Mum and her boyfriend Kurt was in Oak Bay. It was one of a long string of similar-looking bungalows. It was brighter and roomier than the cottage, but there were no oak trees or hills to climb. My school, Willows Elementary, was nearby, and I spent all of grade three there, graduating in the fall of 1963 when I was eight. Mum always fixed my hair before school, usually in braids with colorful ribbons. My school was a very old building with wooden floors that shed splinters into my arms and legs when I fell. I discovered that some of the teachers were fond of using rulers to control their young students.

One sunny day in class I was chatting with George, who sat next to me and who had red-brown hair and green-blue eyes and the best smile. He was left-handed like me and drew wonderful pictures with pencil crayons. I leaned over, my long braids dangling, lowered my voice to tell him a joke, and he giggled. Crack! The teacher had quietly walked up behind

George and brought the flexible yardstick down on his hands, right across the knuckles. He bowed his head over his hands and cried—quietly to avoid another strike—and I nearly fainted with fear.

According to my grade three report card, my performance was better than average with schoolwork, but I had relational problems with other students at times, and I talked too much in class. An earlier report had said I had trouble concentrating, unsurprising given my home life. My recollection is that at each new school either I or Janie would be teased and sometimes bullied, which led to me arguing and squabbling with those students. One social challenge I faced was that I spoke with a slight British accent and used British pronunciation for words, which led to me being regularly picked on or laughed at by kids at school. That is why I adored George. He was always kind to me and never made fun of my accent; he listened to my stories and showed me his colorful artwork.

In our house in Oak Bay, there was a special room that began to fill up with things. There were boxes of ornaments, exotic paper and fabric flowers, tiny sailing ships, and other interesting knickknacks and objects wrapped up in crisp, brand-new paper. When I asked Mum about it, she excitedly told me that she and Kurt were going to open a store; she was going to call it The Trading Post, and this was their merchandise. It would be a gift shop and trading company with things for sale from around the world. "It will be fun, and you can come visit after school and help," she exclaimed, putting her arm around my shoulder and hugging me to her. The affection was delightful and a new adventure sounded grand, but I was secretly sad that Kurt had to be part of it. I desperately missed my kind father as my sister and I continued to endure unpredictable cruelty from Kurt, who I thought was the meanest person in the world.

In this house, as in the others we had lived in, my sister and I shared a room. It had a good-sized window that was bright in the mornings and looked out over the backyard. Janie was an early bird. I was not. She loved to wake up and patter over to my bed and hold my face in her hands while whispering my nickname, "Gee, Gee, are you awake? Time to get up!" I would pretend I was asleep but, being just a breath away from my face, she didn't buy my possum act. She massaged my cheeks. I could usually smell cereal on her breath and knew she'd been in the kitchen, moving quietly as a mouse. If I squeezed my eyes shut, she would try to peel them open. Sometimes I giggled, and sometimes I was grumpy and pushed her away. The main thing was to be really quiet. If Janie spilled anything in the kitchen or we laughed too much or dropped a toy on the polished floor of our bedroom, there would be "hell to pay" according to Kurt. We knew he wasn't kidding.

President Kennedy was shot in 1963 while we lived in that house, and I remember standing in front of the television engrossed in the black-and-white scenes and the distraught people on the screen.

In one of my final memories of that house, the door to the special room full of treasures for the Trading Post was ajar. As I peeked in, there among all the boxes I saw large duffel bags leaning against the wall. I saw something odd. Poking out of the top of the bags were the barrels of guns. I recognized them because Grandpa had a rifle in Dawson Creek that he used to hunt rabbits. I found Mum and asked her about this new addition to the room. She startled me by weeping profusely, then closed the door and told me never to go in there again. As she walked down the hall, I suddenly got the shakes and went to my room and very carefully closed the door.

CHAPTER 10

angels

As a survivor of childhood abuse, most of my clearest recollections are experiences sharpened by deep emotions of pain or joy. Sandwiched in between the extreme memories are layers of ordinary days that take some effort to remember. Still, there were normal and gentle times, like bike rides, birthdays, card games, hopscotch games, and bedside prayers. As I gently pried open these more typical early memories, they unfolded into moments of sweetness.

Occasionally when we were little girls, Mum would come to our room to tuck us into bed. She would sit on one bed or the other and talk to us in a gentle voice. When it was my turn to have these few lovely minutes with her, she would settle on the side of my bed and stroke my hair and talk about the day or perhaps what she was planning to do that would be fun for us. Her hands felt warm and reassuring, and I breathed in her perfume as it floated by my face. Her soft, sweet words were like a caress. I wiggled a bit closer, snuggling next to her and wishing she would not leave but just stay and stroke my head. As a girl I invested so much hope in these tender moments, even though I knew from experience that future plans were never reliable.

After this memory emerged, a rhyming prayer that Mum taught us popped into my mind and I called my sister to see if she remembered. She did, with very similar words. Instead of the word *night*, she remembered *fears*. Perhaps each of us had our own special version:

> Four corners round my bed,
> four angels round my head.
> One to watch, one to pray,
> and two to keep the night away."

Soon enough, Mum would again be gone from our lives.

CHAPTER 11

embroidery

"Mr. Goldie!" My grandmother's very British voice sailed down the polished aisle until it struck Mr. Goldie with full force. He had nowhere to run. But I did not know that he might have been inclined to seek shelter. Six months after another move that I don't remember, Mum and Kurt were gone, and I was accompanying my grandma to the local grocery store in James Bay, an area of Victoria where she lived. In those days, anybody important at the store wore a starched white coat, and the really important people had their names embroidered above their breast pockets. Mr. Goldie was the manager, and, in my eight-year-old opinion, had the best-looking jacket in the place.

As Grandma descended upon Mr. Goldie, I was mesmerized by his name, written in cursive red thread. I craned my neck so I could see it better. I was tugged and tucked under Grandma's arm as she plucked away at Mr. Goldie with her clipped British words. "I was here earliah today and purchased a pound of *buttah*. It was clearly marked at 40 cents. But, Mr. Goldie, when I arrived home and reviewed my bill, your *clerk* had rung up 45 cents!! Now, Mr. Goldie, I am not a genius at arrrithmetic (she rolled her r for emphasis), but I know when I have been *ovahcharged*. I trust, Mr. Goldie, that in the future, you will ensure your *clerks* mind their arrrithmetic!!"

As he always did when Grandma launched a crusade, Mr. Goldie paid solemn attention, nodded often with his hands clasped in front of him, addressed Grandma formally, and said just enough to satisfy her that he had carefully listened. Grandma, who had an unfulfilled desire to "be on the stage" as she put it, would assume the appropriate pained but noble expression while striding behind Mr. Goldie to be ceremoniously refunded her five cents.

I thought it was all quite terrific, as we got a good deal of attention in the process and I generally got a candy from one of the clerks. If Grandma saw the offending sweet, she'd exclaim, "Throw it *away*, dahling!! You don't know *who* has touched it and *where* their hands have been." Then, she'd grab her neck and make a choking sound to ensure I could envision the consequences of swallowing a germ-laden albeit wrapped candy.

Living with Grandma was to be a captive of her personality and perceptions of life. The world in her view never had correct manners, was never truly clean, was unable to count money properly, and was decidedly not educated or sophisticated enough. While she frequently sang and danced her way around her kitchen and living room and talked grandly about "the *stage*," she rarely played the rather expensive stereo she had in the parlor. She did have a television and watched a select few programs, with

EMBROIDERY

Florence in the 1960s

the Lawrence Welk Variety Show being a top choice in the early evening, complete with orchestra and classically trained dancers. On those evenings, my sister and I would watch her sail around the living room with Lawrence and continue waltzing with her tea towel around the kitchen table the next morning.

How we ended up living with Grandma is another woeful chapter in my family history.

CHAPTER 12

all the right doors

In late 1963, Janie and I found ourselves living at Grandma's house, where we stayed until summer 1965. She owned an old Victorian house, one of a row of homes from that era, all perched colorfully along a road that led to the sea. She never had a driver's license—for which the world should be grateful—and converted her sloping gravel driveway into a rock garden that tumbled over with flowers in the spring. An enormous peace rose bush grew up the south side of the first floor, displaying an extravagance of peachy-pinky-cream blooms that were unreservedly fragrant all summer. Passersby would stop to take photos of her cheery house with the neat black trim and gingerbread fittings, surrounded by a compact but gregarious garden.

She probably never planned to have two of her grandchildren living in her partially finished attic—the only place to fit those little beds that had been taken from our father's house and trucked 2,500 miles to Dawson Creek, then moved 800 miles to Victoria where they eventually migrated from apartments to houses to Grandma's. Our room was furnished with the two beds, two dressers, an area rug, and a chair or two. A large chimney from a no longer used fireplace ran up through the center of the room. Victorian homes were quaint but rarely practical for family comfort.

My memory of this move begins at Grandma's house, very relieved that Kurt appeared to be out of the picture, asking Grandma where Mum was, why we couldn't go back to our house in Oak Bay, and could I keep going to my school.

When we arrived at Grandma's house, we were both already attending a private school. I was in grade four when I was eight, and Janie was in a split kindergarten/grade one class at six with the mean teacher who bashed her knuckles. We had cute uniforms, and I had lots of friends and enjoyed being outdoors as often as possible during lunch break. We finished up the year there in summer 1964 when we were nine and seven, and then Grandma enrolled us at James Bay Elementary in her neighborhood. I was quite disappointed to leave my private school and complained, but Grandma said it was "terribly expensive" and that I should "go to public school like other children." Each day that we left for our new school I held Janie's hand as we went down the steps onto the street and walked the few blocks to the entrance. Grandma would follow us onto the sidewalk and stand and watch us until we were safely inside the doors of the school.

Janie and I both liked our new school in James Bay. It was small, and the teachers were kind and helpful. Up to this point my school life had its ups and downs, while Janie had mostly unpleasant experiences. Kids were expected to take part in class, but Janie much preferred her inner world. By this point in her life, she was scared of almost everything.

The secret place she'd made inside her mind was peaceful and full of imaginary friends, and she was happy. She chose quietness as her hiding place. Many teachers had seen her as a daydreamer or lazy or stupid and punished her. Students like Janie who didn't listen had been forced to put on a paper hat marked DUNCE and spend time facing the wall. Or she was slapped. To be in a school that didn't insult or hit her was a great relief.

A teacher at this school noticed I was having trouble seeing the blackboard, even after she moved me to the front row. I was sent home with a note asking my grandmother to take me for an eye exam. Off we went to the optometrist, who had massively bushy eyebrows and announced I was "quite shortsighted." When my new glasses arrived, I was completely amazed by what I saw. The blackboard was no longer a problem, I could see people clearly and stopped tripping over things. For days afterward I stared and stared at clouds, trees, street signs, and magazines at the corner store. For once, being teased at school didn't bother me. I was too busy looking around.

Both Janie and I loved books. Janie read all of The Happy Hollisters and the Beatrix Potter books full of talking animals—Peter Rabbit and Tom Kitten and Mrs. Tiggy-Winkle. I regularly visited the school library and glowed in the attention of the nice librarian. When I was having a bad day and didn't want to be with other kids, I'd go and see my librarian and talk to her about life. She suggested books, and I'd sit there and read my way through lunch break. I longed desperately to be with the characters I met, who all seemed to have normal lives and two loving parents and a dog and went on interesting vacations. If there had been a door to leave my life to be with Nancy Drew or the Hardy Boys, I'd have grabbed my sister and jumped through.

Living with Grandma was fascinating and weird. She washed clothes in the bathtub with a plunger, pounding away with surprising vigor. Thunka, thunka, splurt, splash! Thunka, splash! I wanted to make those sounds and asked for a turn and then was sorry because it was harder than it looked. All year round, she made us brush our hair in a room we all called "the shed," an unheated, unfinished back room attached to the kitchen. Even with Grandma's odd habits, living in this house was the first time Janie and I felt somewhat safe and content since we'd lived with our father. Still, my sister and I often felt wistful and sad, and in the attic we'd talk about our father and wonder where he was and where Mum was, and we'd hope very, very much that we'd never see mean, awful Kurt again. We'd read books until daylight was gone from the one large window in our attic bedroom.

Our life at Grandma's was predictable. We knew she'd be home when we returned from school, or she'd prearrange for us to go to a neighbor's house and wait for her. She was a good cook, and breakfast, lunch, and dinner were served at regular times with food I mostly liked, and Janie wasn't hit or screamed at or sent to bed for not finishing a meal. For full disclosure, I'd become a champion at making Janie's rejected food disappear, which was much easier at Grandma's because she would turn her back to go into the pantry. We adored her baked rice pudding and her bread-and-butter pudding—everything was cooked from scratch.

Another dessert was baked custard served with stewed prunes. For me, the custard was a delight, and I really didn't mind the taste of the prunes. Janie on the other hand was filled with dread at the sight of a prune—so, yes, I ate mine and hers. I was probably the most regular kid in the city.

The only weekly ritual I dreaded was the dose of cod liver oil we each were required to swallow from a huge spoon on Sunday evenings. It was disgusting. I managed to get it down with the promise of dessert, but Janie had awful trouble and gagged and cried. After episodes of her vomiting the slimy stuff all over the kitchen floor, Grandma switched her to vast amounts (so it seemed to her as a little girl) of Ovaltine and Horlicks, a malted barley health drink. Regrettably, I was required to keep swallowing the grim spoonful each week.

Keeping our energetic inclinations under control while inside the house was not as easy for Grandma. "Hoooeeee! Stop that at *once!*" Grandma's high-pitched call pierced the ceiling and reached us in the attic where we'd been leaping onto and jumping off our beds, laughing our heads off and then arguing about something. The door to the attic opened, and we were called downstairs and escorted to the kitchen, which sat directly below our bedroom. That room had a beautifully decorated ceiling, painted sky blue with a special motif that crisscrossed the entire area. Grandma silently pointed up and we saw it—many new and noticeable cracks in the paint. My heart fell because it looked bad. We were sent outside to play for the rest of the day, which Grandma viewed as punishment but we did not.

CHAPTER 13

the news according to grandma

One afternoon I came home from school and there were strangers in the house, which was amazing. Hardly anyone was allowed in Grandma's house and especially not strangers. I was shocked speechless to see several men in suits walking through the house and even more shocked to see that they had their shoes on. Nobody ever walked through Grandma's house without removing their shoes—she would say, "Think of the germs!"

Even more interesting was that they were coming out of the shed with suitcases as well as big bags full of papers. Grandma was not bossing them at all and was actually wringing her hands and treating them like they were in charge—also shocking. She said something like, "I don't have any idea what's in those cases. I just stored them because my daughter Rose asked me to."

As I was gawking at all the activity, a woman stepped out of the shed into the kitchen, stopped and looked at me, and then looked at Grandma. I can't remember what she said, but she gazed at me for quite a while, then her face got sad. I was fixated on her pants. No woman I knew wore pants. If my eyes had got any bigger, they might have fallen right out of my face. At that point I was deeply disappointed to be shooed upstairs by Grandma to our room in the attic.

Once upstairs I crept over to the front windows in the unfinished part of the attic. It was dark and I was scared, but I was more curious than afraid. The men were putting the bags of papers into a car. Janie was upstairs with me but flatly refused to come into the unlit part of the attic to see what was going on. After everyone left, I went downstairs. "Grandma, who were all those people? Why were they taking our things out of the house? And they had their shoes on! Does it have something to do with Mum being gone?"

"Oh dahling, it is so very *sad*," Grandma replied, clasping her hands over her heart and sighing, "Your mother had to go away for a while." She avoided saying anything more specific.

People coming and going was nothing new in my life, so I accepted the vagueness, even with the very surprising and strange visit from people in suits. I continued to be grateful that the nasty and unpredictable Kurt was gone, and I continued to miss my father.

Soon after the visitors had left, I was walking through the living room and noticed a newspaper article lying on the never-cluttered coffee table. Later I realized that Grandma knew I read everything that I found, so I believe she had planted it there for me. The story was about my mother's trial on fraud charges, her conviction, and her jail sentence. I took little sips of air as I read it again just to be sure it was my mum. It was her name, the dates lined up with her disappearance, and there was Kurt's name. My mother. Arrested.

I carefully put the clipping where I'd found it and went to tell my sister.

When I got the courage to ask Grandma about the newspaper story and whether it was true, she replied, "Yes, dahling, it is so very *sad*. Your mother got mixed up with that *terrible* Kurt, so sad." Then she left the room to make a pot of tea with a special treat of sweet biscuits, and after dinner we all watched the Lawrence Welk Show. Grandma did not sail around the kitchen humming songs for quite some time, and we never spoke of the newspaper article again.

One day I got into a fight with a boy at school. I was really, really mad because he'd blocked my way on the sidewalk with his bike then yelled, in front of several kids, that my mother was a jailbird. He and his friends laughed at me. I did the worst thing I could think of, which was to rip my beret off my head and whack him with it. All of this happened in front of the school. Then I took off running for home. The next day, that boy got into deep trouble with the vice principal, and word spread fast that he got the strap, which was a piece of thick leather used on the hands or rear ends of bad kids. I heard about it and was really scared.

When the vice principal came to see me after class, I burst into tears thinking he was going to haul me down to the office to get the strap, too. Instead, as I gulped and shuddered, he told me in a very serious voice that he'd seen the fight the day before and had talked to my grandmother. After the verbal reprimand, to my surprise, I got a solemn pep talk. He told me I had a lot of potential if I could just focus and stop fighting with the boys. "Angela," he observed as he bent slightly toward me, his hands in the pockets of his extra-tall, somewhat baggy beige suit, "You're smart. You can go places in your life." My legs were so weak and shaky I could hardly walk home.

My sister and I have often talked about our mother and the awful truth that she went to jail. But we were always a bit unsure of the details. In 2021 I decided to try an online archival search to see if, by some stroke of luck, I could find any newspaper coverage. I really wanted to validate my memory of reading the clipping. After reaching out to the helpful people at the Victoria Archives, I got some tips on how to search for newspaper articles. In the 1960s, there were two newspapers in Victoria. One of the publications had loaded all of their old issues online; the other had not. It was definitely a long shot. I went to the online archive, and to my amazement, a search turned up one article. I sat for a minute and then went through the entire 24-page edition, finally locating the article on the back page.

The report said that Kurt was to face charges for breaking and entering and theft from a post office. Apparently, he had made a run for it and was found and arrested in northern BC after the police found a large number of checks, money orders, and bearer bonds in our mother's apartment in Victoria. She was also arrested, charged, and remanded to appear in court. My cousin Adrienne, daughter of our Uncle Stewart, is an absolute whiz at online research and found several related articles.

Piecing together the story as an adult, I thought back to the amazing inventory in the special room of our house in Oak Bay and wondered how much of it had been stolen. Maybe all of it, given how hard Mum cried when I asked her about the guns I had seen. Once we left that house, Mum may have asked Grandma to take me and my sister, or we may have moved once more to a house in James

Bay where Mum was living when she was arrested. I then realized that those men and women in Grandma's house were detectives.

When I found the newspaper article in 2021, I was both relieved and sad to find proof that my memory was correct. When I called my sister the next day with this news, we concluded that while we lived with Grandma, our mother had been sent to Oakalla, at that time a state-of-the-art prison for women that focused on rehabilitation. Generally, the women who ended up there had short sentences of less than two years. Given that our mother had originally been charged with breaking and entering, was living with the man who committed the thefts and then pleaded guilty to cashing multiple forged money orders and possessing more that she knew were stolen, it seemed to us that her sentence was light. However, when we read through additional articles sourced by our cousin Adrienne, the picture became clearer.

Somehow our mother and her lawyer convinced the judge that she was a victim of a cold, calculating man and had been manipulated into her crimes. Kurt was eight years younger than Mum and no genius in our recollections; some days he was barely coherent. The judge roundly criticized Kurt for ruining our mother's life and sentenced him to two and a half years, guaranteeing he would go to the British Columbia Penitentiary, a maximum-security federal prison. The judge described our mother as "cultured, intelligent, capable, and kindly," adding that it was not necessary to send her to a federal penitentiary because "It would do no good for you or your family." Mum went off to Oakalla to serve eighteen months and receive training and support.

Oakalla was later closed and then torn down in the 1990s, but the archival photos of the main entrance, which led to both the men's and women's sections, looked ominous. I tried to imagine my thirty-two-year-old mother being sentenced, and I felt sure she cried real tears. I wondered if Grandma went to the courthouse, and whether she had cried. Then I thought about Mum being driven to that jail as a prisoner and seeing that entrance. She must have been terrified.

CHAPTER 14

shane and pinky

While we lived with Grandma, life had a routine. Except when Grandpa surprised us with a visit. He'd drive up and stretch his tall frame out of his car with his predictable cigar and usually haul out bags of groceries or gifts for us. Grandma would get quite fluttery and bustle around the kitchen making tea and fussing about the cost of the things he had bought. We loved his grocery visits, complete with exotic items such as watermelon, ice cream, and coffee. He never came empty-handed, and his personality filled up all the spaces in Grandma's house.

On one visit, Grandpa emerged from his car with an even bigger smile than usual. Janie and I were stunned when he produced a puppy. Elated, we both wanted to hold the golden lab pup, and I am sure some arguing ensued because we both adored animals. The pup was so soft, full of wiggles and licks, and we both lost our hearts. As the days went by, we settled on calling him Shane and lavished him with affection, taking him for walks—probably with me bossing Janie, arguing that I was the oldest and got first turn—and feeding and brushing him.

The only glitch was Grandma. She absolutely did not like animals, especially dogs and cats. The dog was not allowed in the house, ever, so he was relegated to the shed—the unfinished, unheated, and poorly-lit room attached to the kitchen at the back of her home. It was where she kept her root vegetables, firewood, suitcases, hairbrushes, housecleaning mops and brooms, and gardening tools. And now the dog.

When we were at school, Shane would be chained up along a small run on the side of the house where the ground was covered in large pebbles. I always looked forward to seeing his head bobbing up and down in excitement when I got home. I'd hunker down and give him scratches on his head, hugs and pats and generally smother him with love.

It had to happen. I got home from school one day, and Shane was gone. Not on his run. Not in the shed. I ran up and down the block, searching and calling his name. Then I ran in the house and asked Grandma, "I can't find Shane! Have you seen him? Did he run away?"

"The paperboy has him," she said. "It's better that way." Then she walked back into the kitchen and clattered around with the dishes. Some days I would see the paperboy ride by on his bike with Shane running by his side. Every time, my heart dropped into my shoes with sadness.

At another point during our stay with Grandma, we acquired a female kitten, which my sister desperately loved and named Pinky. The little black and white fluff ball with a pink nose also was not allowed in the house but was assigned to the shed and spent a lot of time either underneath its floorboards or outside. We discovered that while Grandma did not like dogs one bit, she hated cats. If she saw Pinky, she would kick out at her and say something like, "Bloody cat! *Filthy* thing!" I think we had this pet for just a few weeks.

My sister was looking out the window into the garden one day and saw Grandma come around the corner of the house with a broom in one hand and the kitten clutched in the other, well away from her body. At first, Janie was happy to see that Grandma was holding Pinky and thought maybe the kitty would be allowed in the house. Then she realized that her grandmother was heading for a small but deep pond at that side of the house.

Janie watched in horror as Grandma dropped Pinky into the pond and shoved the kitten down with the broom. Pinky never surfaced, even though my sister watched for a long time after Grandma walked away. Janie didn't tell me about this until we were adults. She said that she had nightmares for years, often accompanied by bedwetting. That led to her getting into trouble at Grandma's house and to even harsher punishments from Mum later on.

CHAPTER 15

waiting for mary

At Grandma's house, going out to see a movie was so special that I can only remember one trip to the cinema when we lived there. Most likely it was a rare event because she did not like paying for a show when we could watch them free on television.

The original Mary Poppins was released in the mid-1960s and I probably—though I don't remember—begged and pleaded for the chance to see it. Whether I was able to persuade her, or perhaps more likely Grandma wanted to see her all-time favorite British songstress Julie Andrews on the big screen, we actually went to see it in downtown Victoria.

It must have been fall or early winter because Grandma wore her coat with the silver fox collar along with a pair of kid leather gloves that reached halfway up her arms. I always liked to stroke her hands when she wore those long gloves because the leather was as soft as the fur on her coat. "Dressed to the nines," we called it back then. At the theater, Janie and I were beyond excited and had a hard time settling down in our seats. Grandma was, of course, the only woman wearing a fancy coat in the entire place. I don't think she cared that fashions had changed and people no longer wore finery to the movies. She kept the coat on her shoulders for the entire show.

Sitting behind us was a gaggle of lanky boys who were, of course, behaving just like boys. In those days moviegoers could bring their own snacks, and these boys had brought bags of grapes. The boys rattled their bags, talking, goofing around, and sniggering. Grandma first gave her signal sigh and shoulder shrug, indicating that she was miffed, then glanced behind at them in annoyance, making the passive-aggressive disapproving moves my sister and I had come to know so well. The boys seemed inspired to behave ever more badly. With the movie underway, my sister and I slowly sank lower into our seats with embarrassment as Grandma finally took them on directly and told them to get some manners and be quiet. Then she huffed back around in her seat, carefully adjusting her fur, muttering under her breath, "Guttersnipes, absolute *guttersnipes!*" One of the worst of her insults. They kept giggling and rustling, but much more quietly.

Finally, my sister and I were lost in the show, marveling at the music and the flying nanny who showed up just at the right time with her amazing carpetbag that produced everything at the moment it was needed. I felt like I knew the brother and sister who had lost their mum and lived upstairs in a creaky house with an uncertain future. Mary was just what those two lonely kids needed, with the right amount of sass, magic, and kindness. She sang her way out of problems and had bizarrely funny friends, including a singing, dancing chimney sweep. I learned how to say, spell, and sing supercalifragilisticexpialidocious in her honor.

Janie and I were both sad when the nanny flew away for the last time and the magic was over. We hovered as the credits starting scrolling and the lights came up. Grandma hustled us out of the theater, exclaiming about all the filthy people and who knows what kind of germs they had and that we were going to march straight home where we would *wash our hands*. Once we were outside, Janie looked up at Grandma and asked what was on her collar. Grandma immediately brushed at it and, lo and behold, her glove was sodden with sticky, wet grape seeds. Every time those boys ate a grape, they flicked the seeds right into Grandma's luxurious collar. They had remarkably good aim. The silver fox collar was covered with them. Janie and I did our best to appear very serious about this high crime as we struggled to keep up with Grandma's enraged stride all the way home.

Grandma parked us on the front porch to watch her remove all the grape seeds and mourn the state of her beloved coat. Then we went inside, where we were scrubbed free of lurking theater germs, and it was time for bed. Up the squeaking stairs we went, Janie hanging on to my pajama bottoms because the stairs were too narrow and winding for us to walk up side by side. She never got over being terrified of sleeping in the attic. At the top of the stairs, we always paused for a moment to gather our courage, hold hands and scamper across the unfinished portion of the attic into our room. We had to move quickly because Grandma waited down below by the only light switch for the stairs. We dawdled once, and Grandma flicked off the light leaving us in the pitch dark. Our shrieks of fear convinced her to turn it back, and we galloped to our room where we had a light switch. Thankfully, after that she always called up the stairs with a one-minute warning.

Once Grandma realized that Janie was an early riser and would come downstairs in search of some food, she began locking the door to the attic with a small hook-and-eye to stop her from rummaging in the cupboards. But it also stopped Janie from using the bathroom. My sister would often wake up with a full bladder. Trying to wake me up was difficult as I was a heavy sleeper, so she would muster all her courage and creep across the dark, unfinished room and then down the narrow winding stairs. Then she would bang on the door, begging Grandma to open it so she could use the bathroom. Sometimes Grandma would unlock the door, but sometimes she didn't.

What made our room at the top of the house special was the window. It was built right into the sloping Victorian roof, like a skylight and could be propped opened with a piece of wood that slid in place. I don't remember if we pulled over a chair or stood on the dresser, but I was able to get that window open and could lean out, touch the shingles and see across the neighborhood. I would look as far as I could and wonder wistfully about Dad and whether he was looking for us. It was entirely prohibited and dangerous, but looking over rooftops and trees and driveways was delightful for both of us. Janie's head would just reach far enough for her to get a view, and sometimes I'd lift her so she could see more.

Recently we were reminiscing about the magical Mary Poppins and the boys in the theater and laughing about the grape seeds and Grandma's outrage. Janie asked if I remembered looking out the window, and of course I did. Then she shared something I'd never known. "I kept watching the sky every night, to see if Mary Poppins would come and rescue us. I finally realized she wasn't coming."

CHAPTER 16

my special ladies

One day while I was playing around the front yard of Grandma's house, I saw a couple of neat and tidy older ladies knocking on doors in the next block. I waited to see if they would come all the way down our street to the next-door-neighbor's house. The owner, Mrs. Canford, was rarely seen, and when she did appear, her face and hands were always pale and papery looking. Her dilapidated home had lost most of its paint, and the garden was totally overgrown. She was a source of fascination for my school friends, who all believed the house was haunted and that Mrs. Canford was a witch. My sister and I were not convinced, because Grandma took us to visit Mrs. Canford. Her voice was sweet, and she said kind things, even though her house was dark and dreary and she had a wart on her nose. After one visit I asked if our neighbor was a witch. "Pffffftt!" Grandma replied, "Don't be silly! Of course she's not."

The two ladies did knock on Mrs. Canford's door, and as I eagerly watched, her ragged curtains twitched a bit, but she didn't answer. After they slowly retreated down her uneven stairs, I made sure I was visible when they turned my way. "Hello dear," they called out to me, "would you like to come to Sunday school?" Immediately interested, I ran over to them, asking where it was and were there other children and what did they do and did they have snacks? The ladies were nice, and I told them I wanted to go but we'd have to ask my grandmother.

They smiled and stepped up to knock on our door. I didn't expect a good result because we weren't allowed to do much out of the sight of our grandmother, and none of our young friends were ever allowed in her house. ("Think of the *germs*," she'd cry with a dramatic wave of her hands.) When Grandma opened the door, one of the ladies said something like, "Hello! We're here to invite youngsters to Sunday school, but first may I say what a lovely garden you have. Pointing to a tree that was Grandma's pride and joy, she asked, "How do you get your camellia to bloom so much? Mine barely has any flowers." An intense discussion about tea leaves ensued.

My grandmother explained that she threw used tea leaves on her camelia tree, adamant that they made the plant thrive. Yes, I nodded, anxious to be included from my spot on the stairs. I thought back to the many times I'd seen her fling those soggy tea leaves with feeling, and I'd be riveted as I watched them drip and droop and slide down the trunk to the ground. Some days, she threw with a little more emphasis. Sploosh! Every year the bush produced glorious salmon-colored blossoms that lasted a day or two then fell to the ground in a skirt of glistening, heavily ripe petals. The tea got all the credit, as it did this day in the chat with the ladies.

To my delight, I was permitted to attend Sunday school. I'd also been allowed to go to Sunday school in Dawson

Creek, which had been fun at first, but I stopped going when two girls in my class were nasty to me. I was hoping this time would be better, and it was. Someone would stop by to pick me up each week. Once we arrived at church, I'd run downstairs to the basement to see who was there, greet my special ladies, and take a quick look at the snacks. I enjoyed learning new songs with clapping and gestures and hearing stories and watching another lady play the piano. The ladies were always thrilled to see me, and my ten-year-old self soaked up their attention and their warm hugs. Grandma was kind to me in her own odd fashion, but she was not a hugger.

Soon enough, we'd be moving—again without warning—leaving behind my ladies.

CHAPTER 17

a rescue mission

In the fall of 1965, a car drove up and parked in front of Grandma's house. I was on the front porch tending to the flower boxes. To my amazement, my mother bounced out of the car, ran up the steps and gave me a hug. I was vibrating with excitement. "Mum, Mum, Mum!" I yelled. Janie came running to the front door. "Come on then," she exclaimed, "pack up your things. You are coming to live with me in Vancouver!" We ran in the house, laughing and talking, and Janie and I raced upstairs to the attic to get our things. Just like that we were waving goodbye to Grandma through the back window of the car. She waved from the porch, then from the sidewalk, and then she stood in the street still waving.

We rode the ferry from Victoria to Vancouver, and the whole trip was a grand adventure. I don't recall asking where Mum had been for the past year and a half. By then I was ten, and Janie was eight. Mum, now thirty-three, asked us a lot of questions about living with Grandma, and we answered as fast as we could, vying to tell our stories. She was not happy that Grandma cut our previously long, thick, curly hair to just above our shoulders. Mum stroked our hair, joked with us, and poked fun at Grandma's eccentricities. I was thriving in the limelight of Mum's attention and regaled her with stories about Grandma's legendary frugality, how she checked her receipts every night down to the penny while a cigarette hung out of the corner of her mouth and Janie and I held our breath, waiting for the ever-lengthening ash to finally crash onto her paper and coins. As someone who never found a dollar she could not spend, Mum roared with laughter.

Janie told the best story about "the buggy," and I likely interrupted her numerous times, claiming my privilege as the bossy older sister. We all knew that Grandma used a small wood stove in her kitchen to keep the back of the house warm because it was cheaper than turning up the gigantic old furnace. Janie recounted how we would often trek the six blocks down to the James Bay seashore following a storm, trailing after Grandma. She would briskly march along pushing a very old baby buggy with a metal frame to collect driftwood for the stove. Sitting on the ferry with our mother, we all tumbled into giggles as Janie described the three of us seaside foragers trooping along with the rusty buggy screeching mightily in Grandma's grip. I mimicked the noises, "Eeeka! Eek, clack, eek, eeka!"

At that point, I could not contain myself and interrupted with my own version of the story, about how I had fun running around finding pieces of wood and bark that were the right size. But the best part, I exclaimed, was always when people passing by wanted to chat. During either stretch of the journey to the shore or back home again, women would occasionally stop us and want to "see the baby." Admiring babies in buggies and strollers was a common practice at the time, a sort of public celebration of family. Perfect strangers would lean across the buggy, smiling broadly, perhaps asking, "Oh, let me take a peek! Lovely! Is it a boy or a girl?" Janie and I would stare silently at the women in anticipation. Without fail, their startled heads would pop back up after coming face to face with a pile of smelly, sand-streaked flotsam. Grandma never spoke up or tried to stop them, her philosophy being "People should mind their own damn business and serves them right!" After these encounters, she would march off with us in her wake, muttering "Silly *fools!*"

Mum laughed and laughed about the buggy. "Your grandmother is dotty—absolutely as flaky as pastry!"

Then we told Mum that we were never allowed to have friends over, no parties or cakes for birthdays or for other special occasions. There were one or two gifts each—usually something practical like shoes or a scarf and perhaps a book. We had a lot of rice pudding for dessert, and once a week we had baked custard and stewed prunes. Janie made a desperate face when I mentioned the prunes. If we were really good, Grandma treated us to a cup of weak tea and biscuits. Visitors were rare when we were home from school. There were occasional visits from Grandpa and one or two friends of Grandma's who sat in the parlor, which was off-limits to us, sipping tea from the best china cups while perched on a silk-covered loveseat. Nothing was out of place in the house, except for the contents of our room in the attic; cleanliness and order was the supreme state of Grandma's bliss.

Mum stroked our hair again and put her arms around us and declared, "I'm taking you away from all of her weirdness! She is so boring! We are going to have fun! Parties! Trips! Ice cream! I smiled, my memories of our past with her already fading away. I just knew it was going to be better this time!

When we arrived in Vancouver, I was surprised when we moved in with Grandpa. He was living alone on Broadway near the Kitsilano district in a three-bedroom townhouse that was furnished nicely but without frills. My sister and I got one spare bedroom, and Mum had the other one. Autumn was turning to winter. The city felt colder, darker, and much, much bigger than Victoria. There was far more traffic and more people, more houses, and so many apartments. It was a lot to take in.

I was tall for my age, but standing next to Grandpa I felt decidedly short. He was well over six feet tall, had the stomach of a man with a passion for food, and dressed with flair. He had a big smile, a big laugh, and his big temper

Grandpa in the 1960s

was still intact, though the full force of it was reserved for Mum. Grandpa loved to eat in nice restaurants, and every now and then he took us downtown for dinner. Our eyes boggled at row upon row of stores and neon lights and then at all the choices on the menu. Like Mum, he was a happy spender and left impressive tips while puffing spectacularly on fat cigars.

Not long after we moved to Vancouver, I began to miss Grandma. I tried to sort it out in my mind. Yes, she was odd and never let us have friends over and hated dogs and cats (I hadn't known then that she'd drowned Pinky) and was scared of germs and locked us in our attic bedroom. But she never hit us, and never yelled or screamed. And she was always there waiting for us, every morning and every night. She took us to the beach and let us play for hours in the sunshine. In our new home, we let ourselves in after school because Mum and Grandpa both worked. One or the other of them was often out in the evening. We didn't get to have any parties or to invite any friends over. And there was the shouting.

Mum and Grandpa still argued and fought. It wasn't bickering that started small and kept growing but more like sudden outbursts and explosions. During one verbal detonation, I learned that Mum was on probation, which she hated. I found a dictionary and looked up "probation" and figured that she couldn't afford a place just for the three of us, so she was stuck with her father and we were stuck with her. I often wished that we were back with Dad and that I could play cards with him in the living room. My hope began to trickle away.

Mum enrolled us in yet another new school. I preferred my smaller school in Victoria. This new school was in a huge building, crowded with students, and it was a much longer walk from home. Janie and I walked to school together—I was responsible for looking after her along the route—and we had to cross a busy road with traffic lights and then walk eight blocks. My first report card from General Gordon Elementary School said I was capable of doing better work. However, by the time I graduated from grade six at age eleven, I ranked high in my grade, and the teacher remarked that I got along well with everyone.

CHAPTER 18

silver bells

Mum got a job in a flower shop, and I was entranced by her creations. She was attending floral design school and made amazing bouquets. She worked with a group of mostly older women who all fluttered around Janie and me when we came to visit, making a sweet fuss. They would play with our braids and tell us how pretty we were and remark to each other how well behaved we were. We felt special because they let us into the back of the store where we could watch them whip up a glorious flower arrangement in what seemed like seconds. I was deeply impressed.

One of the floral designers, Penny, constantly had a cigarette hanging from her mouth, reminding me a little of Grandma. Back then, many people smoked at work, including in the back of the flower shop. With her gravelly voice and squint, Penny seemed tough but was always kind to me and my sister. I never got tired of watching her arranging flowers as she smoked and drank endless cups of coffee and Coca-Cola. She was wiry and arranged flowers faster than anybody. She seemed hardly to look at the vase, talking, selecting flowers, cutting stems, hands moving, cigarette smoke around her head, and suddenly there was a spectacular bouquet sitting on the counter.

The owner of the store participated in a program to give women who were on probation or somehow in trouble a chance to rebuild their lives. She ran the design school and supervised her employees at the store. She was a chain-smoking, no-nonsense woman who wore her hair in a bun. She, too, was always happy to see my sister and me and spoke sweetly to us. Reflecting on this now, I wonder what would have become of my mother (and the two of us) without this lifeline.

Penny kept a silver flask on her work bench. I was very curious about it and found out why it was there in December, an intensely busy time for flower shops. All that month when we visited after school, I saw her sipping from her flask as she raspily crooned a few lines from the song "Silver Bells," swaying slightly as she thrust flowers into vases. Her creations never seemed to suffer from her indulgences, and I learned all the words to that song.

I was fascinated with the whole scene: the all-women environment, buckets of bright blooms, spools on the wall holding dozens of rolls of ribbon in every shade and hue, the smell of the flowers, the fragrant pine and spruce branches at Christmas, the phone constantly ringing, the ring of the front door bell as customers came and went, the telex machine dinging and then pounding out orders from other towns, and the huge glass-doored, walk-in fridges stuffed with color and cheer. Mum smiled and laughed and worked very fast. She seemed to flourish at the flower shop, and I began to feel hopeful for calm ahead and maybe even our own place.

CHAPTER 19

tiny lions

Penny and Mum became friends. For a period, I spent quite a bit of time at Penny's place and got to know her family. Once in a while I was thrilled to get permission to stay overnight. When I visited, Penny would bustle around at home, still absorbing remarkable quantities of Cokes and coffee, a cigarette dangling as she spoke out of one side of her mouth. She seemed to never stop moving. She was a single mom, and the light of her life was her son Jake. He seemed so tall and mature and polished to me; he was probably in his very early twenties. Jake was nice to me, and I liked him, but I was completely smitten by his buddy Manuel. I had a severe crush.

Penny lived on the main floor of an apartment building and let me play around outside, making me check in with her often, or she'd look for me out the window. I happily puttered out there and only came in when Penny made me. One day by the front entrance, I discovered a litter of fluffy feral kittens in the shrubbery. The mother cat was half-wild, tame enough to cadge food, but those kittens were fearsome. I would stick my head in the bushes and their fur would puff up as they backed away, their eyes wide and wild. I spent hours trying to win them over with food, but they hissed and spat and retreated into the depths of the roots and branches, watching me with glowing eyes. They looked like tiny, growling lions and I really wanted one. They had other ideas, and so did Penny. I begged and cajoled, but there were not to be any ferocious kittens in her tidy apartment.

One day Penny asked Manuel to give me a ride in his car. He actually opened the car door for little tomboy me, and I had a princess moment. The car had cream-colored leather seats and a stereo, which in those days was the height of luxury, at least from my perch in life. Usually curious and chatty, I was awed to the point of one-word responses to Manuel's gentle questions. I kept my head down, overcome with an unusual bout of shyness, but I watched everything through my bangs. All these years later, I still remember how I admired Manuel's dark, well-groomed hair, trendy 60s clothes, the Burt Bacharach music on the stereo, the amazing car with the butter-soft seats, and his courteous ways.

I adored Penny like an auntie and would gladly have moved in with her, tucking myself in a corner somewhere out of the way so I would be safe, to watch her life and hopefully become part of it.

As I recall, Mum later had what she called a "falling out" with Penny who soon disappeared from our lives. I was deeply sad about the loss of my friend and her kind ways. If I asked about Penny, I would get a vague dismissal, "Never mind about her." I got the same response when I asked about our father, but angrier and with threatening stares.

CHAPTER 20

departure

One evening while we were living at Grandpa's place, there was an eruption of tempers that blasted us into a different orbit.

Grandpa and Mum got into a fierce argument in the kitchen. Janie and I retreated to the living room, my sister hiding behind me as we stood at the far end of the couch. I tried to be brave, hanging onto the arm of the couch to steady my legs. I could see into the kitchen, but from a safe distance.

Grandpa's shouting seemed to bounce off the walls and reverberate through my chest. From what I could make out, I pieced together that Mum had not come home the night before.

What I learned in the aftermath was that Mum loved to walk along Kitsilano Beach and sometimes went there after work or floral design school. I am sure she found it a place where she could sit on a stranded log and look out over the watery expanse of English Bay, probably feeling older than her thirty-four years and hoping for a better future. In those days, there were still seashells to be discovered on the butterscotch-colored sand and pretty agates and sea glass to collect. Sometimes she'd bring a little bit of the beach home to us, and I'd put the treasures in a jar in our bedroom. Every now and then she would take us on a walk to the beach, about ten blocks each way.

On one of her visits to the shore she met Frank, who liked to beachcomb after work. They formed a friendship, and then this one night she stayed over or fell asleep or somehow did not end up back where and when Grandpa expected her.

Grandpa alternately yelled at Mum, then growled at her shouted replies. She cried and screamed. I shuffled to the back of the couch, my head and shoulders visible. He was angrier than I had ever seen before and finally bellowed, "If that's the way it is, then you can get out!" He was sitting at the dining room table and swept his hand toward the living room. "*All of you just get out!*" Peering over the couch, I felt smothered by the rage, and Janie was clinging to my waist, her face buried in my back, her entire body trembling. He looked directly at me, my face likely a mix of terror and panic, and then turned back to Mum who was finally silent. He shouted again at his daughter, "Get out!!"

I was almost eleven and Janie was nearly nine. It was a watershed catastrophe in my young life because I was old enough to realize that our own grandfather was tossing us out onto the street and we had nowhere to go. My legs went weak.

Mum came into the living room and got Janie and me under each arm. We ran up the stairs to her room and all sobbed together on her bed. She clutched us close and cried that she was so sorry. We packed our suitcases. Grandpa did not change his mind.

We carried our things out into the street. The shaking in my legs had stopped and now I was simply numb, walking woodenly away from our home. I was relieved to hear Mum say that we had somewhere to go and it wasn't far. We walked to Frank's small house, about three blocks away on Balsam Street. Mum moved into his room and we girls shared the other bedroom. That night, I heard her brokenhearted crying through the wall.

I soon learned that another woman with a young son had lived with Frank before us. They left behind a black cat, and we were thrilled to have a pet that went by the name of Queenie and was mostly cantankerous. I was secretly pleased that this move did not require a change in schools, so I continued through grade six. Frank had a car and didn't mind driving us around, which was a huge treat, and on the weekends we started taking day trips to the beach and parks and other interesting places. We had a picnic cooler with sandwiches for lunch and thermoses of tea and biscuits. Once in a while, we were treated to ice cream cones.

After Mum had graduated from floral design school, she was usually home when we arrived from school. She cooked regularly, and the meals were tasty. Her pies and pastries were delicious. Both Mum and Frank loved music and played the latest tunes on his stereo, singing or dancing or both. Junk food was readily available, including chocolates and other candy, frozen desserts, and potato chips. Frank was also a British immigrant, so the cupboard held his favorite snacks from home. Our lives became more predictable, and we seemed to always be going somewhere now that a car was available. Janie and I disappeared into our room when Mum had a migraine or was in a bad mood; her temper was still very much intact, and trouble was never far. While in that house, I can remember getting several beatings from her that made me scream.

Mum sometimes told me to walk to Kits Beach with my sister after school to meet her and Frank. It was a long way, about fifteen blocks. We'd find them on the grass or the beach, soaking up the sun after work and with a big picnic cooler of food. The beach had a saltwater pool that was filled by the tide, and along the back seawall there was a stage called

Angela just after moving into Frank's house, age 11

the Kitsilano Showboat.[1] During the summer we would sit on the grass above the pool and watch song-and-dance routines, magicians, and talent shows. Janie had learned to sing, and one night she was part of a singing competition and placed second; we were so proud. We were having adventures and life was looking up!

But a nightmare was hiding, soon to pour its darkness on my hopeful heart.

Janie just after moving to Frank's house, age 9

CHAPTER 21

off to the suburbs

In the summer of 1966, I was eleven and graduated to grade seven at General Gordon Elementary in Vancouver, and Janie progressed to the next grade. By October, we'd moved to Bridge Street in Richmond, a suburb outside Vancouver where Mum and Frank bought a house on a quarter acre of land. The blue and white house was comfortable and bigger than Frank's house in Vancouver.

Downstairs held a double living room, a generous kitchen attached to a sunny family room, the bathroom, and the master bedroom. Upstairs Janie and I each had our own room for the first time, and for some odd reason there was a tiny sink under an alcove in Janie's room. When Grandma came to visit, she was thrilled to wash her hands each time she went upstairs. Our family acquired an undisciplined spaniel puppy who remained a free spirit, plus a couple of female cats who were not spayed and became kitten factories.

All of the lots in our neighborhood were large, and everyone had vegetable and flower gardens, pets, sheds, greenhouses, ponds, and more. A few small blueberry farms were tucked into the landscape. The neighborhood was made for kids, and there were plenty of us roaming around.

By this time, Frank was less friendly and began to pick on us verbally. Just as with Kurt, Frank had rules for no apparent reason, and breaking those arbitrary rules resulted in verbal abuse. I avoided him as much as possible, mostly by finding any excuse to be out of the house. He was somewhat less nasty when Mum was around, so I tried to time my presence with hers. Summers were better because we could be outdoors for hours, no questions asked. And we spent part of each summer at Grandma's in Victoria, where Janie and I enjoyed every day with her at the beach.

Janie and I enrolled at Garden City Elementary, where my grade-seven report card stated I had adjusted favorably to my new school situation. I made a friend there, Peggy, who remains in my life to this day. Peggy showed me that the spongy, peat-based ground at the back of our property would undulate when we jumped up and down, so we spent hours back there, two gangly girls, leaping around, falling down, and laughing hysterically. During summer, we got odd jobs picking blueberries or strawberries at nearby farms where we consistently got into trouble, usually because I was goofing around. I loved those times when I felt like a normal kid doing normal things with a normal friend.

When I told Peggy I was writing this book, I shared a few stories about my mother. She was genuinely stunned, because Mum had been unfailingly kind to her, inviting her for dinner, giving her gifts, and encouraging her friendship with me. Peggy was Mum's favorite friend of mine, ever. The part of my mother that Peggy experienced was the polar opposite

Far left Peggy; far right Angela, grade 7

to her own stepmother, so she became attached to Mum and carried positive memories through the years. Frank, however, was always rude and unwelcoming toward Peggy, so she had no trouble understanding my desperation to stay away from him. Both my mother and Frank were usually charming and funny outside of our home, especially toward adults they didn't know well.

I graduated to grade eight at junior high school, and Janie moved up a grade. Mum lived with Frank and adopted his last name, but they did not marry. Janie and I still had our father's last name. Frank joined a scuba diving club, and our family enjoyed many weekend trips to beautiful coastal spots where we kids explored the shoreline and Mum visited with the divers' wives while Frank swam the watery depths. Frank continued his work as a furniture mover, and Mum opened a small retail store in the mall on No. 3 Road. Then I entered grade nine, and worked part time for Mum at her store.

We were more comfortable financially, and Mum showered us with gifts on special occasions. But Frank was getting nastier, and Mum's volatile nature still hung over us like a thunderstorm on the horizon. While we lived on Bridge Street, navigating unpredictable family dynamics became increasingly complex and risky. One day, Mum came home from work in a rotten mood, so we kids knew we were going to be in for nastiness one way or another. Pretty soon she grabbed a large wooden spoon from a kitchen drawer and came after Janie, who was about eleven years old.

The reason for this episode of unfettered rage is gone from my recollection. She had become deliberately sadistic about beating Janie: She wouldn't stop until my sister cried. Janie, exhibiting a bravery I never possessed, refused to cry. This particular beating went on and on, as Mum hit my sister's slender body repeatedly, until Janie fell down next to the kitchen table. She struck anywhere she could, head, back, arms, legs, feet, rear end. Full force. Janie crawled partway under the table to get away from the beating and finally started to cry. But Mum did not stop.

It was a horrible and traumatic beating that brought back my early toddler dread of the kitchen table. In that moment, I was stuck, unable to move, living and breathing a terror that had immobilized me. I was big enough to stand in between them, and I did not. I was afraid.

Finally, Frank grabbed Mum's arm and said, "That's enough." I was stunned that he stepped in because he was so horrid to us. Mum stared at Janie and spat out something like,

"Stupid, *stupid* girl!" Frank pulled her away. What I wanted to do in that moment was to grab that wooden spoon and hit my mother's face and hands with it. But I couldn't move.

Janie was still under the table and stopped crying. She must have been in shock, but neither of the adults tended to her. I hope I helped her up a flight of stairs to her bedroom, but I don't remember.

What I do clearly remember is that I felt like a coward, not unlike the cowardly lion from the Wizard of Oz, except no one brought me along a yellow brick road to bestow on me the gift of courage.

Time Travel

The smell of fruit
shifts me back, back,
squatting in fields hot and ripe
picking strawberries for pocket money
with my best friend.

Our transistor radio rests in
the warm dirt, blaring the best of the day.
We sing along, loud and happy,
to Herman's Hermits, The Monkees,
The Hollies, The Beach Boys.

Part of me wants the money,
but most of me wants to laugh and dance
and jump, scattering energy and angst.
To be normal. Oh, to be normal.

We cannot resist temptation,
hurling overripe orbs at each other.
Splat!

T-shirts bloody red, baskets only half full,
the picking boss glares at us.

I leap across the rows and we are banished.
Grabbing our bikes, we run and gasp,
doubled over with teenage hilarity,
pedaling back, back.
She to her beloved father,
icy stepmother, and unkind sister.
And me to my house of pain,
clutching the day to my heart
like a compass.

CHAPTER 22

tentacles

I don't remember the first time. Or the second time. Fear blurs days and months and even years together in the mind of a young girl.

Not long after we crash-landed at Frank's house in Vancouver, maybe a few weeks later, he started cuddling with me on the couch. Sometimes Janie would be on the other side of him, but most often I was alone. For a lonely girl who was naturally affectionate and clasping tattered memories of a kind father, it was special. Along with couch time, he gave us ice cream and played boisterous music so we could laugh and dance. Mum would laugh and twirl us around to the music, flashing her electric smile as we giggled and spun.

He was always willing to watch me when Mum went out, which was becoming more frequent. A built-in babysitter was a gift for a mother who loved to be out and about.

Then one day on the couch watching television, one hand started quietly roaming around my eleven-year-old body. I froze in place. Each time that Mum went out after that, I begged to go with her, to go to a friend's house, to go out and play. I spent hours thinking of ideas to get out of the house. Sometimes I was lucky, sometimes not.

I would be trapped on the couch with the hand. The fingers. Always moving, claiming, insisting.

Gradually, he started a long process of increasingly cruel insults and put-downs meant to crush me by inches.

Mum regularly told us in ominous tones that if we ever said anything bad about our family outside of our home, especially at school, that the police would come and take us to a home for juvenile delinquents. "Don't trust anyone," she would say, "because they want to take you away!" By then I was desperate to have a home that didn't disappear. In my kid's mind, what I had was safer than waking up to yet another disruption. I believed her and kept silent, even as his abuse and her beatings continued.

During the next couple of years, my body developed and those fingers knew every change. Then his tongue was in my girl's mouth, reaching and choking me. He forced my hand onto his hard penis and rubbed it up and down. He raped my mind and polluted my puberty. His verbal abuse picked and chopped away at my teenage self as he made fun of my clumsiness when I stumbled over my fast-growing feet, and joined Mum in mocking me in falsetto tones when I would cry. Eventually he settled on a nickname for me: Ugly. And that is how I saw myself for many years.

I started working outside the home as often and for as long as I could—baby-sitting, and after we had moved to a less urban area, fruit picking, then helping Mum in the back of the retail stores she worked in and managed, and eventually owned. Anything to stay away from the house and out of Frank's reach. I told my mother I did not want to be alone with Frank, and she just laughed it off, calling me ungrateful and too emotional.

He sexually abused me in every house we lived in. When we suddenly moved from Richmond to Tsawwassen, I lost my school and friends. But the hands were always waiting for me when I was alone in the house. On my breasts, in my pants, everywhere. I learned how to disassociate, to just exist. My reports cards at high school were dismal, and I barely graduated from grade twelve. By that time, I was a walking column of anger, resentment, and fear.

I did not know I was being wounded and scarred for life. I did not know that the constant assaults on my mind, body, and soul would leave dark shadows that haunted me for years and imprinted anxiety in my lexicon of emotions. I did not understand that my mother was both enabling this abuse to happen and amplifying it with her own physical and mental abuse. I did not know that I would be ostracized by Mum, Frank, and Janie when I left home and then shunned again when I started to talk about the abuse. I did not know that I would carry a lifetime fear of bullies that is almost incapacitating.

From the time I was eleven years old in Vancouver until I left home at eighteen, I was just a kid trying to survive.

CHAPTER 23

underwater

A sudden move from Richmond to Tsawwassen when I was in the middle of grade ten brought us into a practically new two-story house. It was by far the nicest place we'd ever lived. Janie and I each had our own bedrooms; there was a spacious living room, a separate dining room, and a sunny kitchen that opened onto a big deck. When Janie and I were home alone, we would race up and down the hallways and stairs, trying to bean each other with socks from the laundry that we were supposed to be folding. The house and neighborhood definitely felt upscale for us, with plenty of room for teenagers to stretch their legs.

Downstairs had a fully finished basement with a big family room, complete with a bar, and extra rooms. Frank wasted no time stocking the bar, and he and Mum would regularly throw big parties, usually for their many friends in the diving club. Reflecting about that time as adults, Janie and I realized that we'd both been sampling the bottles in the bar after school, then watering down what was left. We laughed and laughed about that.

By the time we moved into our beautiful new house, Frank spoke only reluctantly to either Janie or me at home, except to bark orders at us or berate us for eating too much food or not keeping our rooms clean or dragging our feet across the floor, or whatever else might irk him on a particular day. Just like Kurt, he made arbitrary rules and punished us constantly. He would call me "ugly" and Janie "stupid," and then cross his arms with a smirk on his face.

When Mum was in a good mood and announced that I had received a high grade—by now increasingly rare—or admired some artwork of Janie's, Frank would simply grunt. If Mum pressed him, he might say something like, "Yes, that's good, but it doesn't change all the trouble they get into." If she pressed him more, he'd pretty much always say, "I don't go in for all that soft soap." It was dumbfounding to me; when he was outside the home, he never met a stranger. Same thing when he hosted parties and when visitors came over—he talked and laughed nonstop and was the friendliest guy on the block. Everyone seemed to like him.

Laughter was almost always allowed at home. Mum enjoyed making fun of other people and was very good at mimicry, and we rewarded her with guffaws. Sometimes Janie and I would dress in goofy getups and parade around the house talking in fake accents, trying not to laugh but usually dissolving into giggles. By then we had two dogs, a miniature poodle and the spaniel we'd acquired in Richmond, and they too would be costumed in whatever clothing we could get on them. Everyone would watch as the dogs desperately tried to remove the clothes by rolling around, galloping up and down the hallways, shaking one leg in the air, and on and on. The whole family would laugh uproariously—even Frank's shoulders would shake at the dogs' urgent antics. When Frank was in a really good mood, he'd feed Trigger, the spaniel, a spoonful of peanut butter, which was unfailingly funny as the dog's tongue went in every direction, trying to grasp and swallow the sticky mass. Often Janie and I would laugh until we cried—a welcome release for our teenage emotions.

The poodle got his own revenge. Mum called him Bijou, saying he was her little jewel. That was before he learned to grab her pantyhose in the morning and race away with Mum pounding after him yelling, "Come back here you little rotter!" I'd be in my bedroom and turn to see him running by at full tilt, the pantyhose flapping above his ears like competition flags. He also would quietly thieve one sock or one slipper from Janie or me and hide those somewhere in the house. We loved him anyway.

Happy times came and went. We took family drives on the weekend, especially to diving spots. Janie and I grew up around the diving club, and we had no end of fun with the other families. There weren't many other children, but we didn't mind. Janie and I would chase each other around with big chunks of bull kelp, playing whack-and-run. Most club members were young adults, and they had the energy to laugh and kid around with us. There were overnight trips too, with bonfires on the beach and laughter and sea salt-saturated hair. When I turned sixteen, the dive club gave me a scholarship to diving school. I became the first teenage girl in the history of the dive club to pass all of the exams and the water test, earning my certification as scuba diver. I was super proud and everyone made a fuss of me. Even Frank said a few nice things.

Always a water baby, I joined the divers for their undersea adventures. To my astonishment, Frank took a lot of time to teach me about diving safely in open water and was consistently nice to me in that setting. He became my diving buddy and would watch over my equipment. In the more remote locations, he'd help me clamber over barnacled rocks into the sea with all my gear. Once we were at a comfortable depth, he took me around and showed me all of the saltwater life in the club's favorite spots. Swimming along slowly, I'd take it all in. Floating weightless in that underwater world, I saw brightly-colored fish, quirky octopuses, hilarious swimming scallops, giant sea ferns, beautiful sponges, and so much more. Being underwater filled my mind and heart with wonder. Once a fat harbor seal zoomed around us with curious eyes, and I was astounded by its speed. We were never far from other divers, and I enjoyed it immensely. It was also one place I felt reasonably safe around Frank. He could not sexually assault me in that environment, in or out of the water, especially with all the club members around. It felt almost normal.

CHAPTER 24

flower doctors

Mum had sold her store in Richmond before we moved, and once we had resettled in Tsawwassen she opened a small flower shop. She had an undeniably creative talent, and it was the perfect outlet for her. She designed all manner of bouquets, finding new ways to enhance and celebrate the beauty of flowers. She created window and shelf displays, always impressing me with her sense of color and style. I moved through my teenage years in that shop, learning how to work at the counter, answer the phone, and make bows and small arrangements. I swept the floors and loaded bowls with vermiculite pellets so the flowers could be arranged and stay stable, unaware of the asbestos risk.

Enid worked in that little shop for my mum for some years. She was an older lady, always well-groomed with salt-and-pepper hair in a French twist, and she held herself with dignity. When she moved around the shop to get flowers or serve a customer, her feet tapped and glided along the cement floor. I thought Enid was an absolute lady on all accounts and concluded she must have been to finishing school because she walked toe-heel instead of heel-toe. Enid always called me "my dear." "How are you today, my dear," she would say as I arrived after school. The phone would buzz. and off she'd glide, toe-swish-heel, toe-swish-heel, toe-swish-heel, reaching in her smock pocket for a pen to take an order, answering the phone in her best professional voice. Florists all wore smocks in those days, a kind of jacket to keep their clothes from getting mucked up with sap and flower stains and water. They were rather like the doctors of flowers.

Enid kept a bottle of pills in her smock pocket, and every day at lunch she'd take out one pill and place it carefully inside her sandwich. Sitting on a stool for her short break, she'd chew methodically, drinking her tea and then popping outside for a quick smoke. One Saturday I was visiting the store and I asked why she had to take those pills, and she told me she'd had cancer. When I asked what the pills were for, her eyes welled up and she turned away. I did not understand what an accomplishment it was to be a cancer survivor in the 1970s.

She never moved quickly but was always in motion, gliding gracefully on the cold floors. She had a sturdy core but could get a little emotional, especially when reminiscing about her past. For reasons unknown to me, Enid was endlessly grateful for the job in Mum's store. Mum was generous to her employees, giving them nice bonuses and sometimes extravagant gifts. I seem to recall Mum buying a new stove or fridge when she found out that Enid's had quit. Enid would always, without fail, burst into tears at this largesse. But when an employee had been around for a while, and especially once they began to feel like family, they would inevitably experience the other side of Mum.

Once in a while, my mother would tip off the deep end and give Enid a verbal blast, then take off, roaring away in her car, sometimes with tires screeching. There was no rhyme or reason to Mum's fits of temper, so it was hard to know how to improve the situation. If I came to the shop after school or on a Saturday, I could always tell if Mum had fired off one of her emotional missiles, because Enid would be standing in a state of silent woundedness that was familiar to me. I'd quietly ask if she was alright. Enid would gently reach for her handkerchief and dab her soulful eyes and tell me that my mother had been very good to her, overall. She finally had to leave the little shop, not being able to find a workable pair of sea legs to navigate my mother's moods.

I kept in touch with Enid into my early twenties after I moved to Vancouver. I would sometimes take a drive back to my old neighborhood and drop by her compact, comfortable home with its view of the ocean. Being a socially immature young adult, I rarely waited for an invitation, instead just showing up with a smile, all perky and ready to be loved. She usually was happy to see me and would fix me tea and sandwiches. "My dear," she would say, "I heard from my son this week." She would glide around her tiny kitchen, toe-swish-heel, toe-swish-heel, while chatting with me about her family. I missed Enid and wished I could live next door to her.

CHAPTER 25

lithium dream

When I was about fifteen, I found my mother, now thirty-seven, in the darkened living room of our Tsawwassen home quietly sobbing, looking out the window into the night. When I asked her what was wrong, she told me that her life had not been what she hoped and that she'd had a lot of disappointments. She had dreamed of more and was afraid her dreams wouldn't be realized. She might have spoken of her hopes for me—I can't recall. I do recall that she expressed no discernable sorrow over her past mistakes that had hurt so many others. Instead, she wept for herself and her lost expectations.

It was at that moment that I chose, in all of my teenage idealism, to share with Mum that I'd read a book about manic-depressive disorder—it wasn't commonly called bipolar back then—and a new treatment called lithium. I told her that it was possible she had the disorder, and I thought maybe the lithium could help her, that it might even possibly help with her migraines. I had misconstrued her earnest and vulnerable words about her dreams as an opportunity to step forward and try to help. What a mistake. Her tears shut off abruptly, and she turned to stare at me as if I had produced an extra head.

"Are you telling me that I'm a mental case?"

I replied, "No Mum, I just thought that you get so down sometimes that maybe getting some help wouldn't be a bad thing." If there had been ice under my feet, it would have been cracking and groaning. Instead, the ice was in her eyes.

"If anyone is sick in the head around here, it's *you*," she hissed at me. She turned and left the room.

From that day forward, she never missed an opportunity to tell me, and many others, that I was mentally ill. Whenever we argued and I wouldn't back down, her eyes would narrow and she would bring out her trump card, stepping right into my personal space so that we were eye to eye. "You know, don't you, that I can have you committed to an asylum? All I have to do is go speak to a doctor. You are really, terribly mentally ill, crying all the time and so moody." Her favorite nickname for me was Sarah Bernhardt, an actress famous for weepy melodrama. While I was pretty sure I was not crazy, I believed with all my heart that she could convince a doctor that I was. She was that good.

Who Took Your Voice

Who took your voice
with all its tone
and volume
and beauty

of pain
and joy
and expression of you?

Who took your voice
with all its color
and silence
and pauses
of rhythm
and pace
and music of you?

Who took your voice
when you exhaled
to show
and tell of trauma
and secret
and treatment of you?

Did it remain inside?
Was it muffled outside?
Dismissed?
Minimized?
Was it met with contempt
by those with too much to lose
and little to give?

Come now,
one
word
at
a
time.
Like the healed leper

it's time
to take up your voice
and talk.

DAVID TENSEN [1]

CHAPTER 26

the family ghost

When I was nearly seventeen, I got my mother's permission to start dating and managed to have a quasi-boyfriend who used to drive out to Tsawwassen (it was a long way from anywhere) to take me out. Lance was older than me and had a Mini Cooper that he drove like a tidal wave was chasing him, and I loved it.

We'd go out to his friends' parties, to a movie, or to bars with live bands (I was tall for my age and wasn't usually asked for ID), and then Lance would get me home before curfew. We'd park in front of my house and kiss for a bit. One night he noticed that Frank was peering over the fence and watching us from an unlit part of the yard, and he told me I had a really weird family. When I got a call from Lance, Frank would very quietly pick up the extension, and when Lance and I were well into our chat, Frank would interrupt and bark, "It's time to get off the phone!" Unsurprisingly, Lance stopped calling. After finding out that I was not Lance's only romantic interest, I wasn't too sad, but I was furious that Frank was creeping around my dating experience. From that point on, I was careful to keep any aspects of my dating away from home.

At seventeen I'd graduated from high school and was working for my mother in her flower shop and was just beginning college. Mum pushed me hard to enroll in community college, and I was surprised to be accepted. After moving to Tsawwassen when I was in the middle of grade

Angela with date for high school graduation, 1972

ten, I struggled socially in my new school. There were other challenges. For grades eleven and twelve, we were all bussed about ten miles to Ladner because Tsawwassen didn't have a senior high. I missed a lot of classes following a bloody and bruising experience having my wisdom teeth removed, and once recovered, I got mononucleosis and was out again for weeks. It was hard to catch up, I was irate about my home life, and I started skipping school. My closest friend had a car, and we'd head to the White Spot drive-in, eat Triple-O burgers, and chain smoke. We returned to classes only because the vice-principal threatened to suspend us. At that point I gave up trying and barely managed to graduate.

To then find myself in college was startling, but I dug in. Mum paid the tuition, and I found the community college environment less socially stressful than high school. With no bus service at all, most days Mum drove me from Tsawwassen to the college's Richmond campus—about fifteen miles by highway. This routine likely would have continued had it not been for an emotional catastrophe.

A few days after my eighteenth birthday, which I had spent alone, I moved out of our family home. Events leading up to that day had been the tipping point for me. My skipping-school friend, who had just left an abusive home, told me that my parents could not ask the police to bring me back because in the eyes of the law, once I was eighteen I was an adult.

I have always been a homebody. I like to have adventures, but I also have a deep need to be centered in a place that feels like I belong and gives me roots. Looking back, I might have stayed with my family, despite the sexual and verbal abuse, but for one insurmountable wound.

I had decided to become sexually active with a boy my own age. A friend told me it could be nice, and I wanted to know what normal love felt like. So, I had a couple of experiences with a partner of my choosing who was tender and kind to me.

It was hard to hide anything from my mother. Somehow, she found out about my sexual activity. She may have confronted me, and I probably confessed. The resulting tumult was unrelenting. She yelled and cried, and Frank called me a slut and a wench (prostitute). If I yelled back, Mum hit me. Somewhere among the arguments, Frank announced that if I didn't like the rules, I could leave. I immediately filled a backpack and headed for the door, only to have him grab me by the hair and drag me back into the house. Frank was a small but very strong man, and he threw me into the downstairs den. I thought he was going to kill me, but he left the room after telling me how disgusting I was.

Mum took me to a medical clinic and had a long and tearful chat with the doctor about my inexcusable behavior while I was sitting on the exam table. They agreed that I should be checked for STDs. Back home, she and Frank announced that I was no longer welcome at the dinner table or at any family functions or outings. I was banned from joining the family diving trips. I was not allowed to work in Mum's store where I had been taking regular shifts around my college classes. They said I had to eat my meals separately, and I was given my own set of cutlery and dishes that I was to keep away from theirs. I also was assigned my own set of towels and sheets, not to be mingled with theirs. My sister was forbidden to talk to me and was punished if she did. No one spoke to me. I became the family ghost.

I had asked several times since my sixteenth birthday to get my driver's license, but Frank would not allow it. So I was left at home without transportation; I was really stuck because there were no buses in our community at that time. I sometimes got a ride to college from Mum who alternated between a verbal barrage of abuse or stony silence during those trips. On those occasions that she did speak to me, my mother made a point of telling me that I was mentally ill and if I wasn't careful she was going to have me locked up in an asylum. Some days I hitchhiked or got a ride to or from school from a fellow student. Many times, I wept on the phone with my friend who had left her abusive home after being thrown around one too many times by her cop stepfather and was living in Vancouver.

The Sunday after my very quiet eighteenth birthday in 1973, my mother, Frank, and Janie had gone out for the day. I called my friend in desperation and cried in despair at my plight. My friend said, "If you don't leave and get away from those people, you really will go crazy. I'm coming to get you."

And she did. I took a small trunk and filled it with my things. I left a long, emotional note explaining why I was leaving. I don't believe I said anything about the sexual abuse, but I cannot recall. We got in her car and drove away, and I could not stop shaking.

There are decisions that we make in life as a result of an experience or as a result of what we believe will happen if we don't make a change. Some decisions are made for all the right reasons but may come back to haunt us years later. This was a decision I ultimately regretted. I made the decision to leave for self-preservation; my family situation was profoundly wrong and flat-out nuts. I felt like I'd been in the middle of a storm of emotions for a couple of years, and I believed that if I left, things would calm down and be more peaceful at home. Janie did not argue with Mum and Frank like I did. She kept to herself. She subsequently told me she was trying to become invisible. I might have picked up on that unspoken signal, but I didn't.

While I was still living at home, I had asked my sister on at least two occasions whether Frank ever treated her badly when she was alone with him or ever touched her in a way that made her uncomfortable. She always said no. I thought it was odd, but I believed her because back then we didn't keep important secrets from each other. When I sent her the first manuscript for this story, I got an awful surprise when it came back. She had written a note to me in the margin:

> I was eleven years old when Frank started molesting me whenever you were not around. In my bedroom in Richmond with the little sink he'd wash his filthy hands before and after he had probed the most private areas of my thin body. He always made threats afterwards. "Do not tell anyone or you will be sorry! I will kill your sister and then kill your cat!" He put the fear of God in me as I'd already seen one beloved cat killed. I have never told anyone this—until now.

She gave me permission to share her story. I am still working through my grief about this. My sister also revealed that when the abuse started she went to Mum, very troubled about Frank. Janie said, "Mum, Frank is doing things to me that I don't think he should be. I want him to stop." Mum's response: "Don't be ridiculous, you silly child! Frank is a good man. He took you in. Stop *telling stories*!" At that moment, Mum revealed herself as Frank's enabler.

We had grown up with a pedophile who had the access he wanted. It is entirely possible that he chose single mothers with young children for this reason. He knew our vulnerabilities, what would work to keep us quiet, how to verbally crush us into submission. He had a ready enabler in my mother. He had probably abused other children before us. Maybe even after us, much as it pains me to think about that possibility.

If I had known, would I have left home when I did, leaving Janie there? As shattered as I was, I doubt it, but I will never know. A few years ago, Janie told me that when she got home that day with Mum and Frank and they discovered my note, she went into a full-blown internal panic. She ran to my room, saw it was empty of my things, then ran to her room. She had seen me as protection, a buffer, at least emotionally. She said one thought kept going around and around in her head:

I am all alone. I am all alone. I am all alone.

She was sixteen. When I left home that Sunday, I cried during the entire long drive to Vancouver. I worried about my sister, but I did not have the strength to stay any longer; my guilt and pain were crushing. What happened to her after I left is distressingly sad. I am still carrying the sorrow.

 part two

CHAPTER 27

phone calls and pixie cuts

The friend who rescued me from my abusive family home invited me to be her roommate in her grandma's basement suite, and I readily accepted. My first job as an adult was in a pizza place on the night shift so I could continue college. The work was awful. Groups of young men just old enough to drink would come in right before closing and order beer and pizza, leaving huge messes. One night I heard them giggling uncontrollably, and I avoided them because they were always trying to grab my legs or my behind. Suddenly they all left, and I walked over to clean up the table. They'd covered two nearly full beer glasses with napkins, quickly flipped them upside down on the table and pulled out the paper. Inside the glasses were my tips. I gave my notice.

I tried to build a life, between screaming phone calls from Mum and Frank, in which they would alternately call me names and threaten me with the police. My roommate said their behavior was ridiculous, but I was still afraid of them. They put Janie on the phone, and she would beg me to come back, which hurt and distressed me. I had no idea what they were doing to Janie. My college performance suffered, and my grades were inconsistent.

During each assault-by-phone I tried to reason with them and was pummeled with abuse and guilt trips. On a particularly bad call, Mum shrieked into the phone, "*You cannot do this you must come home you are not allowed we are calling the police your sister wants to talk to you don't you care about her how dare you!*"

The drama continued to be funneled through the phone line until I thought it might burst. But I kept saying "No" quietly as my mother's and Frank's voices growled louder and louder. Finally, my roommate grabbed the phone and told my parents that first of all the police would not come to get me because I was an adult and secondly to stop calling. She may have blasted them with a few rude names of her own since she was a fearlessly candid and confident young woman. They stopped calling. I did not go back home. I became the black sheep.

As soon as I could after leaving home, I had my waist-length hair cut into a short pixie style and convinced the stylist to dye the front blonde as I'd seen in a British magazine. I'd gone from salon to salon trying to find someone willing to cut my hair very short. Several had refused, certain I'd come back the next day angry with them. Apparently they'd endured some serious screeching in the past from women who thought they wanted a radical change and then did an about-face. Not me. I loved my new hairdo and felt wonderfully avant-garde walking out of the salon on Granville Street.

I had kept in touch with Grandpa, and for my first Christmas alone in 1973 he flew me out to Ottawa where he was living and working as a statistician for the government. By that time, Grandpa and Grandma had divorced and Grandpa had remarried to Harriet. who was kind to me and seemed like a normal, sweet, older lady. They both liked my hair. It was marvelous to feel like part of a family again.

CHAPTER 28

butterflies and beer

When I returned to Vancouver after visiting Grandpa and Harriet, I began trying out different kinds of jobs to see what fit best. At nineteen I began working for personnel companies, doing temporary administrative work, mostly as a receptionist. I needed part-time work to fit around my college classes, but in late 1974 I quit college after a year and a half of fitful attendance, unable either to concentrate or to care about higher education. I shifted to full-time work and enjoyed going to different offices, meeting new people, and learning how businesses operated.

Eventually, I left my friend's basement suite and moved out on my own, following friends from Tsawwassen who were renting rooms or studio apartments in Kitsilano. At the time, that area was full of large older homes that had been converted into suites, which attracted many young adults. Ever footloose, I rented rooms in different locations across the city, then moved back to Kits.

I wrote to Grandpa and asked for a loan to help set up my first solo apartment. I laid out my case for the basics, such as cutlery, linens, and dishes. He sent me a check for $75 or $100 and I was thrilled. I equipped my home and carefully saved the money and paid him back over time, with thanks. I sent cards to Grandma in Victoria, and she to me, but I was careful to keep my distance from her; I knew she would pass along anything I did or said to Mum.

Grandpa was my family connection, and I wrote to him regularly. Long-distance calls were too expensive. About a year after I asked for the first loan, I wrote to ask for another, this time to get some furniture. I received a scathing letter back, announcing that it was about time that I "stop flitting around like a butterfly" and become a responsible adult. He seemed disgusted, and I recoiled from his harsh message. I kept that letter and didn't write to him again, other than Christmas cards, for several years. He stopped sending me the small birthday and Christmas checks I'd received since childhood. I kept working at temporary office jobs and slowly furnished my apartment with odds and ends and lots of plants.

I adopted a pure white longhaired cat named Pooky, who had to be neutered after some unfortunate odorous spraying incidents on my walls. A few months on, I was thrilled to get a Siamese kitten from a neighbor. I was a little less thrilled when I came home from work one day and found the Siamese hanging from my curtains. Naturally, I called her Monkey. They were both beautiful, and I loved them unreservedly, even as they stared at me insolently and sometimes tried to slash my hand as I petted them. I taught Monkey how to play hide and seek around the apartment, and she rewarded me by eating every fish in my aquarium.

Dating was largely a foreign experience for me. Now that I was on my own, I did not know how to behave around a man who was interested in me romantically and much preferred to hang around in groups without that kind of pressure. Having been a victim of repeated sexual abuse as a child and teen, I also didn't know how to say no to a sexualized experience and sometimes ended up in situations that left me feeling used and depressed.

Occasionally I'd meet a nice man who treated me well, and this included one of my hair stylists. He told me that he had a strong policy of not dating his clients, but he waived it for me. He was tall, handsome, trendy, friendly, and a business owner, and I was so pleased with his interest. I dressed up for our dates and tried to act like a sophisticate.

One fine summer day my dashing stylist came by to collect me for a dinner date. I hopped into his pickup, and we had a lovely evening at a classy restaurant. At the end of our date, he pulled up to drop me off at home, and we chatted about what we could do next as I opened the door of the pickup, thanked him, and said goodbye. I was careful to swing out both of my legs together as elegant ladies do, hopped out, and promptly disappeared from sight. I'd plunged directly into a drainage ditch that I'd forgotten was outside my apartment. Fortunately, it was dry. I quickly jumped up but was still standing in the ditch so all my alarmed friend could see was my head, speckled with dry grass and reeds. I assured him that I was fine, just fine. As I brushed grass off my little black dress, I couldn't help myself: I began chortling at the ridiculous end of my efforts to appear refined. Finally, he drove off and when I got inside, I saw all the debris in my hair and laughed some more. I did not hear from him again, and he lost a client.

Beneath my earnest efforts to understand relationships with men lay a tightly packed core of fear that could flash into anger. Regrettably, my fury usually surfaced when I drank. On the weekends we were in town, my friends and I frequented bars with live music and had a few beers or a glass of wine. I wasn't a beer drinker, but one night a man came over to our table with a beer for me, and I drank it. My friends gave us some space, and I had another beer as we chatted, and then one more went down the hatch. The beer-buying guy had a chip on his shoulder that grew bigger as he drank, and before long we were arguing. Then I told him he was an F-ing idiot and to F-off. He threw a beer in my face. I cussed him out some more and threw my shoe at him.

At that moment, my friends came racing over. One on each side, they hoisted me out of my chair, apologizing repeatedly to my angry tablemate, and half carried me to the door, which was a good thing for two reasons. I was so smashed I couldn't walk, and a bouncer was heading our way. My friends hustled me out, and one drove me home in my car. I never again drank beer and never threw another shoe—or anything else—at a person. I kept my wonderful friends—and my unpredictable temper.

CHAPTER 29

the cost of pizza

While I was exploring life in Vancouver, Janie's goal at home was to be as nearly invisible as possible: keep quiet, follow the rules, blend in, and don't have opinions. She'd seen the results of my disagreeing with Mum before I left home—shouting and threats from Mum and Frank, then insulting me until I cried. At all costs, Janie wanted to avoid the verbal abuse that came with "talking back," which was my habit, and once resulted in Frank slapping me across the face. With this history fresh in her mind, Janie did not want to be shouted at, insulted, or hit.

Janie continued to join Mum and Frank on the diving weekends. One day in summer 1973, a young fellow arrived with a club member. Frank greeted him warmly and introduced him to everyone. When fifteen-year-old Paul laid eyes on sixteen-year-old Janie suntanning on a rock overlooking the ocean, he went over to introduce himself. Janie, however, kept her distance. She was not prepared to trust anyone who knew and liked Frank, and besides, she was dating a university student.

Over time while attending diving events, Janie and Paul became friends. Her suspicions were laid aside. By 1974, they were dating. Paul bought a car and drove miles from his home in Burnaby to see her in Tsawwassen.

Meanwhile, Janie's life with Mum and Frank was more miserable since I'd left. Even though she knew it was risky, she'd begun sneaking out of the house around midnight to join friends at the one pizza place in town. On warm summer evenings, she started going out every week—the friends would all pool their meager resources and buy a pizza and sodas. One night she was sitting with her best friend Shonda and a few others at the restaurant, leaning against a partial wall facing the entrance.

The door opened, and Frank walked in. She froze. He walked toward her and from the other side of the wall, reached over, grabbing her by the hair and pulling her over the top to his side. As she struggled, he repeatedly punched her in the face and dragged her out to his car. As he threw her in the vehicle,

Janie at age 16 in 1974

her head cracked on the window. During the drive home he yelled, "Your mother has been worried sick about you—*you stupid girl*," and he backhanded her across the mouth.

Janie thought she was going to die and she went numb. Frank's voice became distant and hard to hear. Her ears were buzzing, and she was bleeding. All the way home, she was terrified about what her mother would do to her.

Janie's friends at the restaurant had scattered, aghast at what they had seen. She later learned that Shonda's parents had discovered she was missing and called Mum to ask if she was at Janie's house. The adults agreed to start searching known teenage hangouts around the small town. Unfortunately, Frank was the first one to find the kids. When Janie got home, Mum and Frank went into her room and ripped out everything that was special: jewelry, posters, trinkets, books, stereo—they stripped everything that was part of her identity. When they were done, the room was bare except for the bed, an alarm clock, a chair, and a dresser. Frank burned her beloved posters and her stereo disappeared.

The day after Frank's assault, Janie's lip was split, she was bruised all over and had a black eye. Mum had called Sarah, a family friend who was a hair stylist, to "help with Janie's hair." Part of Janie's hair had been ripped from her scalp and the area was bald. When Sarah saw Janie's face and scalp, she hugged Janie, cried with her, and did the best she could. Just a few years older than me, Sarah was in a difficult marriage with a verbal abuser and was trying to survive and protect her small children. While she was working on Janie's hair, Mum's voice was in the background, describing her battered daughter as "horrible . . . useless . . . wicked." Seventeen-year-old Janie was grounded for a long time and was unable to see Paul.

No one called the police to report this brutal assault. When I asked Janie why someone at her school didn't ask about her injuries, she said she didn't go to classes for quite a while. She would walk off in the morning and then circle back home after she knew Mum and Frank had left for the day. She said that her teachers didn't seem to care; Janie had worked so hard at being quiet and unseen, she simply disappeared. I knew from my own experiences in high school that some kids were hardly able to walk after being beaten the night before. One was my friend whose stepfather was a police officer. Kids knew there was no point reporting a beating to authorities; we'd done the math. Exposing our parents and then likely being disbelieved and being sent back home would result in even more abuse. It was not safe.

While I'd known for a few years that Frank dragged Janie out of that restaurant, I did not know the extent of the assault until I asked her to confirm the details. It doesn't seem enough to say Janie's recounting of his abuse appalled me. Before I left, he hadn't hit Janie, but I'm grieved to say that his brutal nature fully emerged, and Mum did nothing to stop him. However, after that night at the pizza parlor, Janie did not remember Frank ever striking or abusing her again.

At the time, though, I was unaware of these family cruelties visited on Janie. I did occasionally hear from my mother, despite Frank's decree that I was not allowed to visit or be part of any family outing or event or to talk to Janie. According to Janie's recollections, no one spoke of me and I'd completely disappeared from the family. But my mother would get my addresses from Grandma and send me a card, sometimes with money tucked inside. She was reeling me back into the family circle, slowly and carefully.

CHAPTER 30

drama queen

When I was nineteen, I thought I was taking another step toward restoring family relations when Mum and Frank finally got married and she invited me to the reception. At the event, he ignored me, so I ignored him. Janie wasn't allowed to talk to me. So Mum was the only one talking to everybody. The event was fittingly dysfunctional, and I knew the door to other opportunities with the whole family group had slammed shut. The estrangement from my sister was a bitter and disappointing outcome for me. I knew it had been orchestrated by Frank and enabled by my mother. I consoled myself with food and ballooned to nearly one hundred and eighty pounds. In photos taken at that time, I am unrecognizable.

The disappearance of my father from my life remained unresolved, and I was troubled about—and sometimes overwhelmed by—my past. I began to experience bouts of the blues. I talked a great deal about my childhood with my friends, who couldn't understand why I didn't have information about my father and why I wasn't allowed to speak to my sister. At times when I felt emotionally sturdy enough, I tried to understand the irrational thinking that had resulted in two young girls being spirited away from their father and why that separation had endured for decades.

Occasionally during my childhood, Mum would make a disparaging remark about me and tie that supposed flaw to my absent father. When I was small and responded with curiosity about him, she dismissed my queries with acidic flares, "There's nothing to know! He was a deadbeat, just useless! Never mind about him!" As a teenager, when I was feeling particularly brave, I would ask for information about him. Her words slashed away at the few tender memories I carried. "He *never* loved you! He was a terrible person! Forget about him!" I would weep in my room, cradling gentle recollections of fireflies and card games.

My inheritance of lies and obfuscation felt much heavier as I entered adulthood. I was working at a government housing office in Vancouver when my first quest for facts led me to invite my mother to lunch. I had been working hard at being an adult, but I was still afraid of her. Her charm at her recent wedding had been delightful, but I was quite sure her temper could reappear and paralyze my mind.

Partway through the meal, I launched into my prepared speech. "Mum, I'd like to learn more about my father."

She appeared startled then said very smoothly, "Your father? What do you want to know about Frank?" She perched her chin on the back of her hand, and she blinked into a shiny smile.

I plunged dutifully ahead, "No, not Frank. My real father, Al. I have some memories of him, and I want to get some information to try and find him."

Her hand fell to the table, a bit too hard. "He's dead. Dead! There's nothing to know. That's it." This new information confounded me, and my eyes wavered on the cusp of tears. I pressed with another question. Her lips were as thin as razors. She looked up at me and down at the table, organizing the cutlery and the cup and saucer and straightening the plate. "Is this how you want to spend your time, you silly girl? Look at you, so *emotional*. I thought you were mature. He's dead. Besides, he never loved you. He always loved and favored your sister Janie. *Always*."

It was some time before I was able to think about my mother's tale in a rational way. After a month or two, I visited my grandmother to ask her what happened and why. "Grandma, I have some memories from when Janie and I were really little. I'd like to understand them better. Why did you and Grandpa take us away from our dad?" Grandma dipped deeply into her personal well of melodramatic inclinations and unique perceptions of reality to deliver her story.

"Oh, my dahling, it was shocking, truly *shocking* to see how you and your sister were being kept! The place was *filthy*, and neither of you were clean. It was *absolutely* unacceptable. You just could not stay there. Dahling, we had to get you and Janie out of there before something *terrible* happened." She put her hands in her lap, bounced them a couple of times, smoothed her sensible skirt, and looked up at the ceiling. "It was all so *dreadfully* sad with your mother and all. So, we took you on a *lovely* vacation. And then your grandfather and I looked after you until your mother was able to be with you again."

"Grandma, what do you mean it was dirty?"

"Oh dahling, you have *no idea* of the filth! None! And there was a woman there, common as *dirt*, supposedly helping him! We just *couldn't* have that." More skirt straightening.

"Mum told me that he is dead."

Grandma huffed and hummed. "Dead?" She continued staring at the ceiling, now accompanied by an odd facial expression. I leaned forward, but she leapt up to make tea and that was that. I wasn't getting anything more from her about my father.

A day or two had passed when I got a phone call from Mum. It was a stream of contained anger. "Did you ask your grandmother about your no-good father? I told you he was *dead*. You must not upset her like this. She is not strong, how *dare* you, if she has a heart attack it will be *your fault*. Don't you dare upset your grandmother. Why don't you grow up and stop *whining* about the past, feeling sorry for yourself? Such a *drama queen*. Just get *on* with your life!" I had to hold the phone away from my ear to avoid the painful screeching.

I didn't know then that my grandmother would be much more forthcoming in the next decade, leading to my discovery that Dad was not dead after all.

CHAPTER 31

the separation

During the wedding reception and then our unfortunate lunch, Mum had failed to mention to me that a big change was coming. I had no idea she and Frank were preparing to move from Canada to the Caribbean.

Janie recalled that Frank came home from work one day and pulled out a map, pointing to three tiny islands sandwiched between Cuba and Jamaica. "I have a job offer to work here," he said, surprising both Mum and Janie as he showed them the Cayman Islands. However, Mum was quickly interested as Frank described his role as manager of an agricultural operation. Janie's heart dropped down to her socks. She did not want to move away from Canada, away from Paul, her friends, and everything familiar. But she had no job, no car, and no ability to see herself living successfully away from the family. She didn't know that she'd been manipulated and abused into believing herself incapable of surviving on her own. Mum and Frank agreed they would try out their new life for a couple of years and see what happened. They made their decisions without asking for seventeen-year-old Janie's input or opinions.

Before long, their arrangements were in place. The house in Tsawwassen was rented furnished, visas were secured, and plane tickets were bought. Mum made some last-minute assignments. Janie and Paul, now reunited after she had been grounded, had to take both of the family dogs to their new homes. The day before Bijou's adoption, the funny and feisty miniature poodle escaped from the fenced yard and was hit and killed by a car. Devastated, Janie and Paul took Trigger, by then an aging springer spaniel, to a farm family that wanted to adopt a small, younger spaniel. When the adopters saw that he was a large, grey-muzzled dog, they refused him.

Janie and Paul found a phone booth and called Mum, who told them to take the dog to the SPCA, which they did, expecting that he would be made available for adoption. After arriving, they were distressed to learn that the only option for Trigger was euthanasia and that they were required to sign papers to make it happen. At that time, old dogs were automatically put down. Both of them cried and then called Mum again; she was clearly annoyed and told them to just get it done. Overcome with sadness about being separated, losing Bijou, and now signing Trigger's death warrant, Janie and Paul wept in each other's arms. After having Trigger for all of his thirteen years and Bijou since he was a pup, neither Mum nor Frank seemed bothered about the tragic loss of their dogs.

In February 1975, Mum called me to deliver the stunning news that they were moving to the Caribbean. They were soon gone, taking Janie 3,000 miles away from the happiness she'd shared with Paul, and, I realized, from any chance of reuniting with me. Just weeks from her eighteenth birthday, Janie cried all the way to the Cayman Islands, with Mum telling her to stop crying, to shut up and grow up.

Before the family left Canada, Mum closed the flower shop she had operated in Tsawwassen where Enid had been employed and where I'd worked. The store closed under mysterious circumstances, according to Janie when we talked about it recently. We believe Mum had probably not paid her bills, which may have been why she welcomed the move out of the country. In both of her retail businesses I'd observed her skimming from the cash drawer, and I'd also taken calls in the Tsawwassen store about past-due bills. Mum would continue this pattern in all of her future business dealings, cooking the books to stay slightly ahead of creditors. She also got in the habit of borrowing money from family and friends to "get over a bad patch" or for an investment in an "excellent business opportunity." She'd somehow forget to repay those who were kind enough to loan her money, leaving them in the awkward position of asking to be repaid. As I was to learn, she didn't use those loans to pay past-due bills she'd accumulated during those "bad patches."

I felt the ache of being so far away from Janie. Now that Frank was gone, I looked up the diving club and went to their booth at a local boat show. I saw a friend and walked over to say hello. He turned and introduced me to Paul, who was astonished to learn that Janie had a sister. I was equally startled to learn he didn't know I existed and that Janie had been dating him. Janie was so afraid of Mum and Frank that she never said a word to Paul about me. "Well," I said to him with a wry smile, "now you've met the black sheep of the family."

We made a few jokes and kidded around with the others at the booth. I reconnected with my old dive-club buddies and went to several social functions. I got to know Paul, who never stopped loving and missing Janie and always wanted to talk to me about her.

By mid-1975, I'd parlayed a temporary reception job into a permanent job at the government housing office, eventually working in tenant placement. I loved my role and enjoyed many inspiring conversations with my colleagues who were a few years older and had college degrees. They encouraged me to continue my education. The job motivated me to get my driver's license, so I took lessons and eventually got a loan and bought a car from a friend's brother. It was tuned for rally racing, had a dual exhaust system, and I drove like the proverbial bat out of hell, relishing the speed.

My restless, unsettled emotions made me a nomad. In 1976 I flew down to the Caribbean to visit my family after my mother had "convinced" Frank to allow me to come for a holiday. It was great to see Janie again and to feel that I was back in the fold. After I returned to Canada, I ultimately decided to go back to the Caribbean and spend a pleasant and reflective sabbatical with my family. Again, my mother paved the way for me to stay.

So, I left my housing job despite the good pay, benefits, and wonderful colleagues. I sold off my possessions, took my two cats and my savings, and flew off to the Caribbean. On the day of my departure from Vancouver International Airport in November 1976, someone took a picture of me with my friends draped around me while my school buddy Peggy faux wept over my departure. They said cheerily, "You are going to paradise! All that sunshine! Why can't we come? Isn't there room in one of your cat carriers for a stowaway?" I held my ticket and laughed my head off, well-oiled with farewell drinks from the bar.

I don't know why I kept trying to fit into the jigsaw puzzle of pain my family offered other than my constant desire to have a sense of belonging.

CHAPTER 32

paradise

Warm air wrapped around me as I headed for the beach on my 10-speed. Before I arrived in Grand Cayman, I'd lost weight, had grown my hair long, and was feeling good about myself. I didn't have a visa to work, so I had plenty of spare time. I was free to sightsee on my bike, swim, snorkel, and visit the shops in George Town, the capital. The island was only about twenty-two miles by eight miles, so I was able to bike almost anywhere.

When Mum, Frank, and Janie all went to their jobs, I had the house to myself. After breakfast and playing with the cats, most days I would braid my hair, put on my bathing suit, toss on a T-shirt and shorts, then head out to swim and snorkel at one of the various beaches on the island. What a life!

One day I parked my bike, grabbed my mask and snorkel from the handlebars, and strolled to the water's edge. I'd chosen an area not frequented by tourists, so I was by myself. Being careful to avoid fire coral that would burn skin on contact, I waded in. I swam away from the shore, cleared my snorkel, and marveled at the balmy temperature of the sea, its clarity, and the beautiful colors below me. Most of the island was surrounded by a reef, and I'd chosen a spot where the reef was closer to the shore, which meant more undersea life to observe.

I got deep enough to avoid knocking elkhorn or other branching coral—I didn't want to break it or be injured by it—and floated along, taking in the scene below. A profusion of color splashed along the sea floor: corals in jewel tones; orange, green, pink, and yellow sea anemones; purple and white sea fans; bright orange and yellow sponges; and striped, speckled and multicolored fish that flashed and shone in the sun. Every shade in the color wheel was below me.

Having learned my lesson on a previous swim, I avoided floating for too long so I wouldn't burn my back and legs. I swam out a bit deeper to check out some unusual coral, and thought I noticed something in my peripheral vision. I looked to my side, but saw nothing. I checked my location and realized I had a long way to get back to the beach and turned around, kicking along at a good rate. There was that flash beside me again. Turning my head to look, I saw nothing.

Swimming to shallower water, on a whim I turned around quickly. Barracuda—a battery of them—were following me. I kept swimming toward shore, trying not to splash like a fish in distress. The next time I checked, they were gone. I didn't know much about barracuda then, other than what I'd seen in bad movies, but I learned quite a lot when I described to Frank that evening what I'd seen. He told me not to be stupid and snorkel in that area, while Mum became alarmed and her voice went up a couple of octaves as she asked how hard barracudas could bite; I'm sure she was envisioning pieces of her daughter washing up on shore. In the days to come, I talked to a few Caymanians and learned that barracuda were more common at that beach but they didn't usually bother people. I opted to avoid the area.

When I explored George Town, I met quite a few Canadians working at the many banks attracted by the tax-neutral status of the Cayman Islands. I made some friends and enjoyed learning about their work and their Canadian hometowns. Most were on two-to-five-year assignments, so there was a constant flow of people moving on and off the island. With the islands being an overseas territory of the United Kingdom, I also met plenty of British people. Some worked in the banks or in hotels and other tourism-related businesses. Other Europeans hailed from Germany and some from Holland and assorted countries.

Cayman, which is how locals refer to the largest of the three islands, was not heavily populated at the time, with about 15,000 residents and plenty of open space. One of the most beautiful spots was Seven Mile Beach, a stunning sweep of whipped-cream-colored sand and palm trees. I visited only sporadically because the snorkeling wasn't as interesting. That area is still stunning, but the beachfront is now heavily developed.

My sister introduced me to some Caymanians and people from other neighboring tropical island countries, and I mostly preferred their company. They were down to earth and didn't have a slightly haughty attitude like many expatriates, especially the Europeans. I dated a bit and then met Juan, a local man who became my regular companion. He would take me dancing at the hotels, or we'd enjoy a show at the one cinema where I'd stare in fascination at the jars of pickled pig's feet for sale at the concession stand. We saw the movie *Jaws* when it was featured, and I screamed along with the rest of the audience. The beaches were quite empty for some time afterward, and no one was in the water. Except me.

For a while, living on a tropical island felt like paradise. We could pick ripe papayas and mangos in our yard, and fresh fish could be speared for dinner at any beach. Frank left me alone. I danced to reggae music. I wandered in and out of shops in George Town and met business owners from around the world. I don't remember watching television, but I read plenty of books and was a regular at the local bookstore. Mum treated me to a short trip to Costa Rica, where we stayed in a gently crumbling hotel with plenty of staff and few guests. The historic Spanish architecture of San Jose and the lush, tropical ecosystem made me feel like I was on a Humphrey Bogart movie set.

Back in Cayman, the other side of paradise was soon on my radar. Janie warned me about the Manicheel tree that reacted to rainfall by dripping caustic sap capable of burning and blistering the skin. The entire plant is poisonous. And there was the Maiden Plum shrub that if disturbed also released a caustic sap able to burn a hole in skin. I stayed away from any overgrown areas, not only because of ferocious flora, but also because of poisonous centipedes, scorpions, and spiders, along with cockroaches and land crabs.

We were most afraid of the centipedes. They had a venomous bite worse than that of the local scorpions and would render an entire limb swollen and useless. The cockroaches were not venomous but were horror-movie huge and common in wood houses. Land crabs frequently lived around the roots of trees and would seize any prey they could overpower and quickly drag them down into their burrows. Sadly, my sister lost a tiny kitten to their powerful claws. Their migratory routes crossed roads, and their one large claw was said to puncture car tires.

Mangrove wetlands, part of the geography of Grand Cayman, are breeding grounds for a number of species, including mosquitoes. When I was on the island, the mosquitoes were most active at sunset, biting humans and soft-skinned animals without fear or favor and were worse as storm season coated the island in humid, damp air. Incoming storms meant we'd see fogger trucks driving past our house, spewing choking clouds of insecticide. Occasionally we'd also see fogger planes fly over the house—there was no escape from the pesticides.

There were two seasons—pleasant weather with sunshine and storm season. Thunderstorms were manic. Claps of thunder were earsplitting, lightning relentlessly slashed the sky, and the rain poured as though a water main had burst above the house. I'd sometimes sit on the screened porch and watch the epic spectacle, knowing my ears would be ringing the next morning. Driving in a rainstorm was not for the nervous. One stormy day, Janie and I were in her car when the skies released a furious downpour. Our only choice was to pull over and wait it out as thunder shook our vehicle. During another storm when I wasn't with her, Janie's car was struck by lightning that blew out every fuse on the dashboard. She was OK, but the car had to be towed to the shop for repairs.

As the months ticked by, I became restless. I was also tired of the host of skin conditions I developed from constant humidity; rosacea and boils plagued me. Juan started talking about getting married, and then we were informally engaged. Before buying me a ring, Juan insisted that I return to Canada, to compare my homeland to a life living on a small island. I was ready to go. I was running low on money and needed to work, and I wanted to see how I felt about a big life change when I got back home. Juan was very sweet and promised me he'd come for a visit once I was settled.

Janie had drifted away from Paul, both because of the distance and because there was no easy way for them to stay in touch. She had a steady boyfriend, also a local man, to whom she seemed very attached. During the time I was on Grand Cayman, I didn't know that her boyfriend controlled her time and questioned her constantly about where she was every minute of the day. That behavior intensified; he became violent, and she was terrified. While a few of her friends knew she was afraid of him, no one knew what he was doing to her. Perhaps she'd have been more open with me if we had fully overcome the gulf created by years of separation and toxic manipulations by Frank and Mum. I left in the early fall of 1977, oblivious that Janie had become ensnared with an abuser.

CHAPTER 33

true north

When my plane landed in Canada, I was happier than I had expected to feel the cool air of autumn and delighted to see my friend Peggy. I was going to stay with her until I got settled. She lived in a suburb of Vancouver and had a little cottage with just enough extra space for me. We laughed, argued about how to load the dishwasher, and figured out how to share the television and remain friends while living together.

I secured temporary office work and began saving for my own place. True to his word, Juan flew up for a visit. However, my Canadian friends were lukewarm, telling me that he didn't seem like a good fit and that my personality seemed somewhat restrained around him. I began considering our relationship in a new light and thought about whether I truly wanted to live on a tiny island three thousand miles away from home. I told Juan I wasn't sure about getting married and needed more time. He went home sad but hopeful.

Not long after Juan left, I moved back to Vancouver and got in touch with my dope-smoking hippie friends. One or two had become small-time dealers to support their habits. Through them I met a new circle of buddies, and I indulged in a ready supply of marijuana and hash to self-medicate. I'd smoked recreationally before I left for the Caribbean but never touched ganja (marijuana) while in Cayman for fear of being thrown in jail. I don't know why I was afraid of prison there and not in Canada, where in the 1970s possessing even a small amount was illegal.

Juan returned for a second visit, and he hadn't been in town long when I realized I could not and would not marry him. I didn't know how to conclude the relationship. A new friend encouraged me to be frank and offered to be moral support, so I asked Juan to meet me at her place. There I told him, in front of several people, that the engagement was off. Furthermore, I announced that I didn't love him and he should go back home. His look of disbelief and distress did not pierce my heart as it should have, partly due to the sedating effect of all the grass I'd smoked that day. I saw him to the door and went to the living room window to watch him slowly walk away, wiping tears from his face. In no way did this nice man deserve such cruel treatment, but back then I didn't see my conduct and words as cold and heartless. Rather I felt that I was finally discovering my voice.

As I watched Juan walk out of my life, a switch flipped in my mind. An internal conversation ensued. Why should I worry about doing the right thing all the time? I should finally do what I want, as my new friends were telling me. Forget guilt; I wanted to have the fun I deserved. I was an adult and could do what I pleased. It was a pivotal moment as

I justified my self-absorbed state and ignored the emotional wreckage I'd just caused. Unaware that I was following in my mother's footsteps, I could not see that the road I'd chosen was dangerous.

I also remained unaware of the real peril Janie was facing in Cayman. In the early 2000s, Janie briefly shared with me that she'd been left behind on Cayman by Mum and Frank and then had to escape her abusive boyfriend. Recently I went to her to ask for more details. Her story was chilling.

Not long after I had returned to Canada in 1977, Janie took a vacation in Canada, where she stayed with family friends from the dive club and visited Paul. When she returned to the island, her car was parked on the street across from the home she'd shared with Mum and Frank, and it was stuffed full of her possessions. A note on the windshield stated, "You have officially moved out." Mum and Frank were gone. No one had seen them leave or knew where they were.

Janie stayed with friends, then got a small apartment and started taking a night class for her job. Phone calls started coming in from creditors looking for Mum and Frank. Janie replied, "If you find them, let me know where they are living." They had done a midnight flit with bill collectors hot on their heels. Janie found the cats at the local shelter where Mum had left them, and she kept an eye on them.

The apartment didn't last. With her family out of the picture, Janie's abuser became emboldened. He came calling, and when she wouldn't open the door, he kicked it down and her nightmare continued. She gave up the apartment and went to live with a friend's family, knowing she'd be safe from her abuser while in that home. But one night in class, her abuser walked into the classroom, grabbed her and dragged her out. No one called the police. He took her to a secluded area. The violence was unspeakable, and at twenty she knew her life was now in danger.

An unexpected call landed Janie a ticket to Costa Rica, where Mum and Frank had been living. Mum invited her to come and stay. She went, hoping for a reprieve, but after a few months, she overheard her mother talking to a rich coffee merchant about what a good wife Janie would make. Janie immediately packed her bag, got a taxi to the airport, and boarded the next plane back to her other nightmare in Cayman. Given the atrocious treatment she endured from her abuser, Janie knew he would not allow her to leave again; she was certain he would beat her to death. So she bided her time, planning a permanent departure in secrecy.

By 1979 I had landed another good government job, but my personal life was a mess. My weight went up and down, as did my moods. Chain smoking cigarettes and then smoking grass and hash on the weekends left me with chronic bronchitis every winter. Since breaking up with Juan, I'd been in a series of failed relationships with men who also had emotional issues. At twenty-four, I had plunged into a heavily self-destructive cycle.

I wasn't spending as much time with my good friends in the dive club or with Peggy. Instead, I was enamored of the group who were seriously involved in drugs. Some had been on the streets; some had been in jail. I mistook their toughness for strength and felt proud to be hanging out with such cool people. I cashed in my future superannuated pension savings to buy a sports car. If there was a bad decision or mistake to be made, I was usually willing.

Around that same time in early 1979, Janie received a note from a friend telling her that Mum and Frank were now living in Nassau. She tracked them down and called. After

Janie mentioned the cats at the shelter, Mum asked her to bring them and come for a little holiday. Janie put her plan in action. She sold her car by word of mouth and paid off the loan, to which her abuser was co-signer. A friend who worked in that bank handled the transaction and agreed to keep the sale quiet for as long as possible. A travel-agent friend in Canada helped her buy a plane ticket; another local friend drove her to pick up the cats and then to the airport.

Janie was all nerves, shaking and nauseated, hoping that the handful of people who knew she was leaving would not betray her. Finally, she was on the plane, taxiing down the runway, and she sighed with relief, knowing that her island prison would soon be in the past. She looked out the window and gasped. Her abuser's pickup truck was speeding down the one road to the airport, dust flying up from the tires as he careened around a bend to the parking area. She strained to look back, then her heart lifted with the plane as it soared in the air.

CHAPTER 34

the descent

When Janie arrived in Nassau, Mum and Frank did not give her a warm welcome. When the two of them left for the day, supposedly to work, they locked Janie out of their home. She spent her days on the beach near their house. She was so relieved to be away from her abuser and so exhausted that she often slept on a deck chair, only getting up when Mum came to find her. She was five foot six and weighed ninety-five pounds—a walking skeleton. The cats were treated better than her.

Janie sent me a friendly, light-hearted letter from Nassau letting me know she was coming home and asking to stay with me. There was no hint of the dire circumstances she'd survived or of the despicable way she was being treated by Mum and Frank. I wrote back immediately, saying she'd be welcome. When she was strong enough, she flew home to Canada in April 1979, and we brought her suitcases to my apartment. She was still very thin. Only days later, Paul arrived with flowers in hand, and they were soon a couple once again. Before long they got an apartment together and were inseparable. Later that same year, Mum and Frank returned to Canada, no doubt with a fresh batch of creditors chasing them, and set up house in Victoria with the cats. Janie and Paul announced their engagement in early 1980 and made plans to be married that September.

In mid-1980 I quit my very good government job, ended a relationship with someone I actually loved who was an alcoholic, and went back to temping. At loose ends, I became intrigued with an idea one of my friends had for a retail store. Before long, we were planning to open a business, using a little money I'd saved and a bit from my partner, plus generous credit from wholesalers. At twenty-five I was ready for a new adventure.

Throughout that summer and fall, Janie tried to plan her wedding. Mum took control like a commando, making the entire process a living hell for Janie and her close friends who were helping. I was the maid of honor but was entirely unsupportive, being predictably self-absorbed. For example, early in the planning process I insisted that my dress be designed differently than the others and be a brighter color. Then I wanted my flowers to be unique. I don't know why my sister didn't fire me. Reminiscing about that time, Janie agreed that I had been no help at all.

On the day of the wedding, the photos of the bridal party took much longer to take than expected. When we got to the reception hall, we discovered that the caterers had brought all the hot serving dishes but unbelievably had forgotten the food. They had to race twenty miles each way in heavy traffic to collect the food. There was also a mistake with a large vat of alcoholic punch, and by then Mum was simmering with barely controlled rage. Everybody in the wedding party stayed as far away from her as possible.

Finally, Mum decided to start serving the alcohol. One hundred and fifty very hungry people descended on the open bar, slurping up the refreshments. Grandpa and his second wife Harriet attended, as did Grandma garbed in a floor-length gown that would have been perfect in an F. Scott Fitzgerald novel. Grandma got snockered on brandy and sang "I'm Just a Bird in a Gilded Cage" as she waltzed around the empty dance floor by herself while glaring meaningfully at Grandpa.

Mum went to the dance floor a couple of times, grabbing Grandma's arm and hissing, "Sit *down*, mother!" But Grandma pulled away and continued her boozy sashaying, occasionally offering a gentle bow when another inebriated guest would clap. Mum stormed to the deejay and ordered him to start the rock and roll. When Grandma finally admitted defeat and sat down, she insisted on being at the head table with the wedding party, dragging over a chair and maintaining a regal but tipsy pose. I'm not sure who'd have won the prize for being the most outlandish prima donna, but Grandma and I were both in the running.

Outside of not helping my sister plan her wedding, I was busy getting the store open. We did the whole thing on a shoestring budget, and while I had lots of retail experience, starting a business was new to me. My partner had zero retail experience but plenty of ideas. We opened and did well for a short time. I worked without a salary as an investment in the store, and my partner pulled out a small allowance to support her family. Before long I couldn't afford my apartment, so my partner offered me a small room at the back of her rental house. I sold most of my possessions to raise some money and brought my books, a table and chair, a daybed, and clothes to her house. We finally decided that to save the business and invest in new inventory we'd take out a loan. She secured a third guarantor, and we borrowed $15,000.

We loaded up on new stock, brought in additional product lines, ran promotions, and business was again good for a time. We were taking money out of the weekly revenue to supply our drug habits and often got stoned after work, my reward for taking most of the shifts at the store. I was dating a man I'd met through the business, and he introduced me to acid. Depression was now my closest companion. In early 1981, I received a gift of about $2,000 from my grandmother. My mother knew about the money and called me asking for a loan. I told my partner I was going to give my mother the money; she berated me for not putting our business first, so I gave it to her instead. That resulted in screeching calls from Mum at our store.

I'd long been a student of astrology and began exploring seances, astral travel, and other types of new-age practices as part of my ongoing quest for spiritual understanding. I felt confident that a higher power existed but couldn't articulate what I was seeking. My partner and I held seances, sometimes with other people; she read the I Ching, and I shared my studies in astrology and astral travel. The overarching message I kept getting from all of these avenues was that in this life I had to learn from my past misdeeds. Or Saturn was in the wrong house, and I would always have burdens and challenges in life. Or I was a young soul with much to learn. Or there was a change coming in the spiritual realm, and I was in danger of being left behind because I attracted dark energy. Rarely did I ever receive an encouraging message from any of these sources, especially if my business partner was doing the reading.

I kept going to work, but our walk-in traffic had slowed, and according to my partner it was my fault because I had been spreading negative energy in the store. One night I was so down and blue that I parked under a bridge and cried for hours. I'd reached a dire low and had planned to drive up on the bridge, get out, and jump. However, I couldn't muster the nerve. When I couldn't pay the insurance, I parked my car and used the bus. A few weeks later I developed a medical issue that left me feeling desperately sick, and I needed to rest for a few days. At the same time, I was recovering from another bout of bronchitis and felt a perpetual heavy weight on my chest. It was as though I was suffocating.

One day I came home from the doctor, and there were a number of people in the house—my boyfriend and several people I counted as friends. My partner announced that I was too dark a presence to stay in her home. They'd had a meeting and agreed I had to go. Everyone nodded. She also was closing the store because I'd failed. "You're a lost soul, and I tried to help and guide you, but we agreed you aren't learning and have to go," she declared. More nodding. Astonished by what I was hearing, I tried to figure out if this scene was a joke. It was not. My boyfriend glared at me and said, "I don't want anything more to do with you." My business partner had arranged for my now ex-boyfriend to put my few possessions in his van with the help of another man. She demanded my house key and told me to get out. The hate in the room was palpable.

I climbed into the passenger seat, but my ex told me to get in the back with the furniture. When he started the van and demanded an address, it was a desperate moment because I did not have anywhere to go. I had a few dollars in my wallet,

I was so sick and weak I could barely walk, and the impact of feeling so hated had evaporated my tears before they could spill. I'd been rude to my family during the past few months and hadn't spoken to my sister since her first child was born three months earlier. But Janie was my only hope, so I gave him my sister and brother-in-law's address in Richmond, a suburb of Vancouver.

No one spoke during the forty-five-minute drive. When we arrived at Janie and Paul's small duplex, the two men immediately unloaded the van on the front lawn. I struggled out, went to the front door, and knocked. Opening the door, my stunned sister saw me hunched over her railing, gazed at the two silent, angry men dumping my things on her lawn. "Hi," I said weakly, "I need a place to stay for a bit. I know this is weird, but I just need somewhere to rest until I'm feeling better and can work. Just short term."

"You'd better come in," she said, staring at my meager belongings. The men finished unloading, leapt into the van, and sped off.

"What happened, Ang?" my sister asked me.

"I'm sorry," I replied, "I'm pretty sick right now, and my business partner threw me out. I don't have any money, but I'll get back to work as soon as I can. I'm so sorry—I don't have anywhere else to go."

At that point I began to sigh, then the tears and sobs began. Janie got me on the couch with a blanket and I cried myself to sleep. Paul had been traveling for work and returned home the next day. I'd dragged in what I could from the lawn and he found a place to put the rest. They realized I needed help. Together, they cleared out their storage room and made a space for me.

It was January 1982; I was twenty-seven, broke, and homeless.

I lay in that little room for weeks. Janie would get me up to eat and try to talk to me, but tears kept pouring out. Some days I couldn't speak or cry. The only bright light at that time was baby Emily, Janie and Paul's sweet daughter. Happy and cooing, she had a ready smile for her young mother and for me.

I struggled under the weight of the dark baggage I'd accumulated; I'd made so many mistakes since striking out on my own. I felt deep anguish because I believed my soul—the essence of my being that would continue after death—was lost for eternity because my mistakes were unforgiveable. A dark blanket of depression led to more thoughts of suicide. But one night I got up to get a snack and heard a sweet sound. I followed it down the hall and stopped at Emily's room, where the door was ajar. I heard her tiny giggle tinkling around her crib and when I looked closer I realized she was laughing in her sleep. I felt the root of something long lost take hold in my heart. Hope.

CHAPTER 35

farm animals

Janie and Paul didn't know what to do with me. I'd lost any awareness of time and thought I'd been staying with them around three weeks. In actuality, I was at their home for about three months.

My sister and brother-in-law's kindness gave me a safe place to begin recovery, and my baby niece Emily was a solace for my crushed spirit. Very slowly, I climbed out of a dark hole and began to feel a bit better. I resolved to give up drugs and never touched them again. Cigarettes, though, were an addiction like no other, and soon I was on the back steps smoking and coughing.

One day Janie sat me down and told me she'd called our mother, who was coming to get me so I could spend some time on the hobby farm that Mum and Frank had bought in Victoria. I apologized to my sister for my behavior in the past and thanked her for helping me. About a week later, Mum drove up, and we headed off to the Victoria ferry. In the three months I had stayed with Janie and Paul, I hadn't often left their house, so when my mother and I walked upstairs on the ferry I realized how shattered I was emotionally and physically. Being around crowds of people made me feel very anxious.

When we arrived at the farm, I took in a sizable, tidy property with a two-story farmhouse, a cute cottage garlanded with blooming flower boxes, and a recreational fifth-wheel trailer. These living accommodations sat in a semicircle, framed by a graveled area big enough for cars and trucks. There were a few shade trees. Behind those were large greenhouses, and behind them was more acreage that contained a generously sized and fenced chicken run. Dogs ran around the property, and my cats were there, staring disrespectfully at everyone from the back steps of the farmhouse. As usual, Frank wouldn't speak to me.

Mum set up some deckchairs and made tea. She and I sat outside, and I explained I had no money and was still weak, but I was interested in helping out to begin earning my keep. She called Frank over and said that she wanted me to stay on the farm for a few months. Frank replied, "As long as she works for her keep and isn't lazy," and said no more to me. I moved into the trailer on the property and began taking care of the chickens, then took care of the small flock of sheep in the front pasture. Mum made Frank pay me a little, and I kept the cash from the egg sales at the farmstand situated at the entrance to the property. Frank managed the greenhouses where he grew vegetables that he sold at a local farmers' co-op. I asked for a corner of one greenhouse and began growing tropical plants to sell in the small flower shop that Mum had opened in town. I was physically stronger, but every morning when I awakened, I felt a heavy, dark blanket of depression laying on my body.

Just when I was on the road to physical recovery, I contracted double pneumonia with a staph infection and was bedridden for several weeks. For once, I couldn't smoke. My doctor, who was in his thirties and starting his practice, told me in a firm and certain voice that if I didn't quit smoking I would *die*. "It's that simple," he said, staring at me. "You are killing yourself." Rattled, I didn't smoke for a couple of weeks. But I couldn't stop entirely.

A few months went by, and, as I recovered I developed a satisfying rhythm to my days. I worked part time for Mum in her store and did errands for Frank, who had finally started talking to me. I got a car and was able to insure it. However, a phone call subsequently rattled my world. The bank that owned the loan I'd co-signed with my partner and the third guarantor had tracked me down. An amount more than $16,000 was outstanding. My partner had not made any payments after she closed the store, and neither she nor the other co-signer could be found, but because the bank found me, I was liable for the whole amount.

I had to go to the bank in Vancouver and was acutely apprehensive about being back in the same neighborhood where my world had collapsed. In a meeting with the bank manager, I told him I'd been very sick but was recovering and expected to begin working full time soon. I was willing to start payments as soon as I got a job. I proposed making enough payments to satisfy one-third of the amount owing and then revisiting the loan. I held my breath and waited for his response. Surprisingly, the manager agreed. Relieved, I rushed back to the farm, away from the horrid memories and crowds. Ultimately, I received a letter from the manager telling me that if I regularly made payments against the total of $5,550, the bank would consider my part of the debt paid in full. I was grateful.

At the end of 1982, I chose to do better in my life. I kept my life very simple. I searched for a center of meaning beyond my shattered self and broken family. I pulled out my astrology books and gave them up. Then I read more about astral travel, which didn't appeal. If something looked spiritual, I'd read the book. I also consumed all kinds of self-help and counseling books, especially about codependency. A watershed moment happened when I was invited to a church where I met some people who all seemed hopeful and were so kind. There were messages of comfort and grace, which I soaked up.

The first church service I attended was bright, cheery, and boisterous. There was a lot of clapping. I didn't know they were Pentecostal; I just noticed that the music lifted my heart and the people were friendly. I received hugs from complete strangers that day and cried during the slower-beat hymns. I went back again, got more hugs, and heard a message about forgiveness and unconditional love. For more than a year, I'd believed that I was irrevocably lost and destined for spiritual darkness, but here people were talking about Jesus, saying he would forgive anyone for anything. I asked to be baptized.

I held my nose and was gently dropped into a large tank of heated water. When I slipped into the water, I felt a warm light bloom in my chest and as I was lifted up, it was as though all the weight and sorrow I'd been carrying poured off into the water. I gripped the side of the tank and wept at the beauty of the feeling as love poured into my broken heart. None of what I saw or experienced was familiar, but I felt at peace, perhaps for the first time. Services were lively, the preaching was powerful, and the amens were plentiful. I asked God to restore my soul, help me quit smoking, and help me rebuild my life, pretty much in that order. And He did. It was a fit, and I was all in. I never smoked again.

At my mother's flower shop where I worked, the creditor calls started; the worst one was from Mum's bank. She'd befriended the manager and arranged to get a loan, but her payments were sporadic. The manager knew me, and during the last call I took from him he said, "Angela, I'm being seriously compromised here. I feel like I've been taken advantage of." I could hear the strain in his voice, and I apologized profusely, explaining I wasn't involved in the store's financing, and I was very sorry, and I'd leave a message for my mother. At the farm, Frank had sold the sheep, cleared out my tropical plant nursery, and was fighting with his twin brother Walter, who was temporarily staying in the cottage. Late one night they both got drunk and brawled outside—I could hear them from the trailer.

On another dark night I heard Walter leave the cottage and start walking around my trailer, the gravel crunching as I quietly went to the door and locked it. Pretty soon the doorknob turned, and my heart was pounding because sometimes the latch didn't hold; that night it did. The next morning, I found that Walter had left packages of children's combs and toys on my doorstep. I didn't know the meaning of the weird gifts but I had a really bad feeling about the entire episode. Then there was my mother, who had responded to my joy at a chance to rebuild my life by telling people I'd joined a cult and was mentally ill. The time had come to leave.

Once again I found temporary office work, and roomed with someone from church for a while. Then I rented a little apartment in Victoria. In May 1983, I celebrated with Janie and Paul on the arrival of their son Daniel. By then they had moved to Langley, a suburb of Vancouver. Work went well, and by the end of 1983 I was promoted. Church was great fun, and I made several good friends. As for the spiritual teachings, I was thrilled to receive clear instructions on how to live my life. Do this; don't do that. After a lifetime of vague, illogical rules, I was ready for black-and-white living. There were rules about how men were to conduct themselves around women, and I felt safe at last. I believed all of this activity was part of turning my life over to God, as I understood from the Twelve Steps of Co-Dependents Anonymous.

During this time, I did a great deal of reflecting on my life and actions. As I recovered emotionally, I concluded that my anger and sense of victimization were going to consume me. I understood that my mother and Frank were probably never going to be sorry for their part in my suffering. Mum continued dripping poisonous lies and exaggerations into relationships we shared, and her words deeply hurt me. I had some choices to make.

Guided by my reflections on biblical wisdom and the twelve steps, I started by making an honest moral inventory of myself and my conduct. That was tough, and even harder was forgiving myself, asking God to forgive me, and making amends where needed. Then I moved on to my long list of people who had hurt me. Candidly, I had difficulty letting go of blame and bitterness because what happened to me as a child was undeserved and appalling. I *wanted* my abusers and enablers to be sorry. In my mind, they were obligated, but they showed no signs of remorse.

Forgiveness, I knew, was essential. However, I first had to define that action. I looked up the Merriam-Webster Dictionary definition of forgiveness: "to cease to feel resentment against (an offender): PARDON." I liked the word pardon because it did not absolve the offender but instead moved the forgiver beyond the offence. A victim can forgive an abuser without any obligation to be around that person. Each time I forgave, I could decide whether I had to change the relationship. I had choices.

I was in the deep end of the pool and found it was the most difficult and challenging inner work I'd ever done. A counselor encouraged me, and I regularly attended Co-Dependents Anonymous. We had a saying in our CoDA group: "Let go and let God," which meant to turn over our shortcomings to God and ask him to remove our defects. In my thoughts I railed against having to look at my own deficiencies when those around me were obviously much worse people. After countless tears and seemingly endless prayers and struggles, I had begun to forgive and let go of my rage and resentment. Instinctively, without fully understanding all of the steps, I kept going. I didn't see it then, but the wisdom of twelve-step programs is to help participants realize that personal success begins by releasing expectations of others and focusing on the one person we can change and improve: ourselves.

I resolved that my only way forward, to grow and mature emotionally and become a better person, was to live with truth as my North Star and focus on my own issues. The more I looked inward, the more work I found was needed. I recognized that as a young adult I'd been repeating patterns learned in childhood: choosing badly in relationships, moving frequently, not managing money well—the list was long. I started to establish a new normal by learning how to make better decisions. How to respond to abusive behavior. How to recognize good and kind people, and how I could avoid failing the people who were important to me. The heavy blanket of depression gradually lifted, and I began to look forward to each new day.

CHAPTER 36

survivors

By 1986, I had established a good life in Victoria and regularly dropped by to see Grandma, who still lived in her Victorian house on the road to the sea with the garden she nurtured so carefully. My mother finally wore me out with her wild temper and lies: I had distanced myself from her and Frank and was nearly estranged, but I wanted to stay in touch with my grandmother. Managing these relationships was tricky while we all lived in the same city.

Still, I liked to visit Grandma over cups of tea and chat about her life when she was young. She always sat in her cozy armchair in the corner of the living room, feet on the ottoman. I would sit in the nearest chair, on the other side of the French doors leading into the parlor that was now forever bereft of visitors. I leaned on the right arm of my chair, talking to Grandma, always curious about family history, testing to see whether she was in a wistful mood and willing to talk about those days. "Let me put the kettle on *dahling*, and we can have a nice visit," she'd say, walking into the kitchen. I'd follow her out there, chatting away, but she would shoo me back to the living room, insisting that I rest my feet after working hard all week. After I heard the kettle's whistle, out she would come with a tray filled with a boiling hot teapot, teacups, milk, sugar, and biscuits. It was one of my favorite rituals.

Tucking my feet under me I'd settle in, and she would take command of her armchair once again, brushing back strands from the soft bun of black-and-silver hair with the back of her hand. Just thirty-one, I already had a healthy amount of grey hair, while Grandma had none until well into her senior years. She was, as always, tastefully and conservatively dressed in a wool skirt and sweater set. As I dipped my cookie into my scalding tea and leaned toward Grandma, she confided that long ago she had been dating a police officer whom she'd hoped to marry when she had met Grandpa, who completely swept her off her feet. Much later I learned from a cousin that Grandma had a job in a jewelry store next door to an antique shop owned by Grandpa's family and that she had met him there. Later still, I found photos of Grandma with Bert, that police officer, and she looked radiant next to him.

Grandma did not marry Bert the police officer, who was clearly the love of her life. She was very smitten with his station in life and with the idea of belonging to the police constables' wives' society, as she wrote on the back of a photo, perhaps trading gardening tips. She had been the oldest of many children, most of whom were entirely neurotic, so it was impressive to think of her aspiring to do well in this way. But it did not happen. Instead, she married a man who did not love her, had a daughter who did not love her, and then after an unwelcome second pregnancy, produced a son who *did* love her.

The sun shone a few rays into the tall windows of her living room, touching the blue Persian rug that covered most of the floor. I put my cup on the coffee table next to my chair and put my chin in my hand as I listened, knowing that we were going to move into war stories. Grandma told me about World War II and running into shelters with Mum and Uncle Stewart, never knowing if Grandpa would be shot out of the sky. During the war the British Royal Air Force had close to a fifty-percent fatality rate.

She told me about her younger brothers and sisters, two of whom died during childhood. She still felt their loss, and I saw the pain in her face. I asked her if she missed them, and she looked at me sadly and said, "Always. They were such beautiful, beautiful children. I had their pictures put in a necklace so I would never forget their faces." More like a parent than a sibling, I thought to myself. Her parents had been milliners and made hats and gloves. Grandma had wanted to be in theater, but her family would not hear of it. She sighed deeply. The sun had moved around the room and was lightly touching the top of her head, giving her an uncharacteristic glow.

Much later I learned from another cousin that Grandpa's mother had been a costume designer for theater and that many of his numerous siblings and cousins had played instruments and were in bands. I was astonished, because he had never mentioned any of that history and never displayed any apparent musical ability. When Grandma married Grandpa much of her family disowned her, which she implied was because of his theatrical connections. Sorting through family history and photos for this story, I did not find any wedding photos of Grandma and Grandpa. I checked their registered wedding date and the birth of my mother, their first child: six months apart. I did find several pictures of my grandparents laughing uproariously, and some of my grandfather dressed in silly clothes and hamming it up. It seems they shared theatrical tendencies, which became the fuel for the nonstop drama of their fights.

During another visit that year over more cups of tea and biscuits, I shared with Grandma that life was finally getting better for me after the difficult decade of my twenties. I had a good job, better friends, and was happy—after a lot of sadness and struggle. With a quavering voice, I told her the truth about Frank, how he abused me and was cruel to both me and my sister. She was shocked—a little too shocked, I thought to myself, wondering how a shrewd person like her could have missed all the signals—and said things like, "I had no idea! How dreadful! Did your mother know?"

She sat back in the armchair and sighed, looking tired, again brushing back some hairs with the back of her hand. It seemed like an opening, and I decided to go for broke. I said firmly that I deserved to know about my father. Was he dead, as Mum had claimed? Grandma opened up, saying she was quite sure he was not dead. He had worked at Loblaws in Oakville, Ontario, as a butcher. I explained that Janie and I wanted to find him. Her advice was to start in Ontario and maybe someone in Loblaws would remember him. She also gave me geographical information about my father's family in England. My heart was pounding. Finally, I had my hands on something that sounded like the truth.

Either during this visit or the one that followed, Grandma got a bit emotional and told me she felt that she had failed in life. She looked over at me, her face filled with sadness instead of its usual slightly worried but always proud expression. Her words and sudden shift into vulnerability caught me off guard. She was fiercely independent and maintained a very stiff upper lip. She looked up at the ceiling and heaved a terribly sad sigh, folding her hands in her lap. For the first time in my life, I thought she looked defeated, and I had no words for her other than softly saying, "I'm sorry, Grandma." I wasn't going to argue with the truth, at least as far as my early life was concerned. I didn't know how to balance her past mistakes with my love for her, and I left that day with a heart full of melancholy for both of us.

CHAPTER 37

lost and found

I called Janie and recounted my visit with Grandma and how she had insisted that our father wasn't dead as Mum had kept claiming. I told her that I really wanted to find Dad. She did too, but we were both too nervous to reach out. What if he didn't care? What if the stories Mum had told me about him were true? What if he had a new family that didn't want us added into the mix? What if, what if, what if?

By this time, Janie and Paul had established a good life in Langley with their two young children, Emily and Daniel. Paul, who was easygoing and friendly, offered to make some calls. He was willing to be the buffer for us if things didn't work out. Paul called his sister Elisabeth, who was living in England at that time, and asked her to try and find Dad's family who still lived there.

The first discovery came from Elisabeth, whose then-husband had found one of Dad's sisters in Cambridgeshire, northeast of London. Though Elisabeth did not have current information, she learned that Dad was living in British

Columbia and provided some leads to pursue. Meanwhile, Paul had embarked on what he thought would be an impossible task. This is his recollection of the miraculous sequence of events in 1986 that led to his finding our father—a story Paul has told many times since: [1]

> I called the head office for Loblaws in Ontario, Canada and explained that I was looking for employment records for the Oakville store. That office gave me the number for the Oakville store, and I called saying I was looking for Albert Hoy, a meat cutter who had worked there in the late 1950s and 1960s. The manager explained that their employment records did not reach back that far. When I asked if there were any very long-term employees still there who might remember, he paused and then said, "Hang on, there's a guy in the meats department who's been here forever. I'm going to yell," which he immediately did. "Hey Luigi," he bellowed, "You know a guy from the fifties named Albert Hoy?" Luigi yelled back in an Italian accent, "Yeah, he moved to Vancouver to join the meat cutter's union."
>
> Armed with the first hard piece of information I had uncovered, I started calling all the Hoys in the Vancouver phone book. I kept a list of everyone that I had reached or missed, because in 1986 hardly anyone had an answering machine, and there were no cell phones. Nearly every person I spoke to was Chinese. Finally, I gave up and decided to try other avenues. Later, I learned that in fact I had called Al's place several times but never got an answer.

One of my closest friends had worked at Safeway since he was seventeen years old, so I figured he would have contact information for the meat cutter's union. He did and gave me the number. I dialed and got an answer.

"Hello, yes, I am trying to locate my wife's father. He worked for Loblaws in Ontario as a meat cutter, and I think he moved to Vancouver in the 1970s to work at Safeway. I wondered if anyone at your office would recognize his name?"

"What's the name?"

"Albert Hoy."

"Tell me why you want to know," the voice on the other end of the phone asked.

"Well, my wife has been wanting to find him for years. She and her sister were taken from him when they were little. I called Loblaws in Ontario, and someone there said he'd moved to Vancouver and suggested I call your office."

Silence; then the voice said, "Hold on a minute."

A different and brusque voice spoke into the phone, "Hello."

"Hi, my name is Paul Cage, and I am looking for Albert Hoy."

"You're talking to him."

I stared at the phone in disbelief."

Both men were stunned by this sudden turn of events. Paul was not expecting to find Al so quickly and was not prepared for the emotional impact it would have. Our father was completely overwhelmed and took Paul's number, promising to call back. About ten minutes later, he did. Paul gave him a short family history, explaining that he and Janie had been married for six years and had two kids, and that Angela was fine and living in Victoria. Then Paul shifted the focus of the conversation.

He recounted, "It dawned on me that this revelation—of two grown daughters and grandchildren living nearby—might be very inconvenient for Al, who probably had moved on with his life and might have another family. I said, "I have said nothing to Janie about finding you. If this discovery is unwelcome, then this conversation never happened, and I'll tell Janie that the whole thing is a dead end."

Dad responded, "I've never stopped looking or lost hope that we would be together again one day. Can we meet tonight?"

The two men, equal parts tearful and elated, remained amazed that a handful of phone calls over a few days had bridged years of separation. They made arrangements for Dad and his wife Marlene to come to Paul and Janie's place that evening. The two homes were just twenty minutes apart.

CHAPTER 38

cherubs

Dad and Marlene drove to Janie and Paul's home, and a magical evening ensued. Some years after the breathtaking gift of our reunion, Marlene shyly told me she'd written about the experience of meeting Janie, Paul, and my niece and nephew for the first time. After I read her account, I knew it belonged in this story:[1]

> In 1983, I married an orphan—or so I thought. No kids, no in-laws. Al and I enjoyed busy and fulfilling work and a social life with friends and my family. Life was good. Oh, I knew my husband had two kids out there somewhere because he'd told me his story about losing them. That story didn't come to life until the day in 1986 when Al called me at work with emotions in his voice I'd never heard before. "You won't believe it! I just had a phone call!" I could hear the excitement, the awe, the wonderment in his voice as he told me about the call from Paul.

I sat dazed, my body and mind going into my own personal hyperspace. I was there but not there. I could hear my pulse in my brain. One thought kept repeating: my life is over, my life is over. Looking back, I don't really know why I had such a thought, unless it was because we were so recently married. How wrong I was. Life was not over; it just got bigger and better and brighter!

In that one phone call all the long years of searching were over. The time was finally right. Al was ecstatic. His two little girls had come back into his life and one lived just twenty minutes away. The angels were singing, and heaven was happy.

I was not able to receive all the joy and feel the positive emotions right away. For the rest of that day, I existed in a kind of bubble filled with fog. My mind was still saying, 'my life is over . . . my life is over.'

Al had made arrangements for us to go to Janie and Paul's home that evening. We had dinner before we left, but neither of us were truly present. In his mind, Al was already on his way to their house, and I, of course, was in bubble land. I explained to him that we needed to give his daughter time to feed the children and get them ready for bed. Well, that didn't last long. I felt like I was trying to hold back a team of horses. We agreed to drive out to Langley, park nearby, and then go for a walk until we were closer to the appointed time. As we got out of the car, a man came up and introduced himself as Paul Cage. He had an inclination to take a stroll, and there we were. He was so gracious, and his easygoing manner put us at ease too.

Then the Universe created one big symphony of events and emotions that was synchronized and beautiful.

When we got to the house long before we were expected, Janie was not ready. Then we saw two of the most adorable faces staring at us in wide-eyed wonder. We were introduced to Emily, who was four, and Daniel, who was two. I was looking at a pair of grandchildren the same age as Angela and Janie when they were taken from Al. The children were also feeling the new, exciting energy that was swirling around and permeating our beings.

It was love at first sight. I gazed upon these two children and felt that wonderful carefree moment of discovery of new life filling up my heart. Like soft, tickly puppies, only better! These children were so adorable; it was as if two cherubs had decided to don earthly forms and bless us with their presence.

We were a family completed. Strangers still, but complete. A long-lost family, each of us unique with our minds and our bodies in different bubbles—that space we inhabit when emotions are going over the top. We were waiting for Janie, who was still working up the courage to come join us, so that we could begin to knit together.

The time with the two cherubs and Paul was well spent. Paul's calm manner took all the bubbling, surging energy and made a kind of music with it, defusing what could have been overwhelming. He had then and still has the perfect personality and all the right stories for pretty much any situation. And this situation was unique.

The coffee was gone, and Paul went to check on Janie. We chatted and waited. Paul went to check on Janie again. For me, it didn't matter whether it was a minute or an hour. It was the experience of something wonderful unfolding.

Then I noticed Al straighten up. From where he was sitting, he could see Janie as she progressed slowly down the hall. I was able to see her reflected in a hallway mirror. Then she stopped, dealing with emotions that no one else could ever imagine. She was meeting a stranger that she would call Dad.

Al was up and out of his chair and down the hall in a split second. I could only see their reflections in the mirror, but even that was a privilege. I watched in fascination as the images of long-parted father and daughter drew close, recognized each other and embraced. They stayed together for a long time in that hallway. After twenty-seven years, being together was the possibility that had become reality. I felt like an intruder, so I glanced away, only stealing a glimpse now and then to see the beauty of the thing.

If Shakespeare was right and all the world's a stage, then the part I played was one of the best. As a supporting cast member I was close enough to the action to see a glorious reunion. The stage had been set in the most perfect way, and life had come full circle.

CHAPTER 39

reunion

When Janie called me in 1986 to say that Paul had found Dad and he was coming to her house that day, it was the long-sought answer to my prayer. I was swimming through emotions: gratitude, wonder, elation, and some apprehension. I was curious, worried, hopeful, and decided to take some time to sort out my questions and feelings.

What would it be like to talk to Dad again after twenty-seven years? To see him? To be seen by him? Could we rebuild despite what had been lost? What would he think of me, my life, my work, my newfound faith? What was his life like? Could I fit into it? I knew he was married. Would his wife like me?

I was completely awash with questions, and each one brought a different reaction. My emotions became a roaring river, so I took a day to retreat and process, trying to adapt to this new normal.

The next day my phone rang at home. I heard a man's voice and, far more quietly than usual, I asked, "Is this my dad?"

"Yes," he replied, "it's me, after all these years."

My heart pounding, I recounted some memories that I had of him from my childhood and he told me how much he had missed us and had thought about us all the time. He wanted to come to see me in Victoria right away, but I preferred to go to his home on the weekend. I was afraid of being so emotional that I would not be functional, and I needed time to prepare.

My car lit by sunshine, I drove onto the ferry at Swartz Bay, sailing from my home on Vancouver Island to the Tsawwassen terminal on the mainland. Once I disembarked the ferry an hour and a half later, my drive would take me to Coquitlam, outside of Vancouver. After finding a seat, I looked out the ferry window at the seagulls soaring over the deep blue ocean and thought about my last conversation with Janie, who was over the moon about seeing our father. She told me there had been tears and laughter, dancing and celebration, with my young niece and nephew fascinated by it all. Janie was breathlessly happy.

"And he's so *nice!*" she said. "So happy we are back in his life!" And then, "And he has *blue eyes!*" No one in our family had bright blue eyes or curly blonde hair like Janie. I had my mother's green eyes and wavy dark brown hair, even though Mum always kept hers dyed blonde. Janie's eyes were an exact match to Dad's.

I was as thrilled and excited as Janie but also reserved, waiting to see how we all would fit together, how I would feel around my father and his wife. I had learned to be cautious around family and to curb my hopes for happiness. The ferry sailed its watery way through scenic island passages as memories floated around my head. After I had left my chaotic home at eighteen, the decade of my twenties had been tumultuous as I lurched between self-destructive behavior and trying to find a meaningful life and career. I struggled to reach a balance, especially because I was on a constant quest to find a way to make my then-family fit into my life. My mother and her husband circled around my thirst for a sense of home, and they required so much for a little of their favor. Then I would fling bitter words at them and reject them for a time. Yet I always circled back. They were all I had. Until now.

The ferry horn sounded, one of my favorite sensory experiences because it told me I was traveling. I loved to be on the move, going places, especially on the ocean. I caught sight of my reflection in the window and felt reasonably satisfied that I was now a person dedicated to healing and hope, on my way to meet my father. I watched the islands and gulls and boats and sea debris flow by. I'd been on a journey within a journey, and now another one approached, something that promised to be wonderful. I made a decision that I would not drop all of my complicated history on my father at once. I would share my story slowly, see how he reacted, and then continue to open up if the relationship seemed stable.

The purser's announcement to return to our vehicles for disembarking jogged me out of my thoughts, and I followed the crowds down to the car deck. The ferry docked, and I joined the lines of vehicles slowly unloading, each contributing to a familiar and rhythmic clunk-clunk as the tires rolled off the metal car deck ramp onto the paved dock. Heading toward the highway, I rolled down the window and smiled into the warm rush of air.

Driving through the forested suburbs of Vancouver, I knew in my heart that meeting my father would be a huge new door flung open in my life, and my soul rejoiced at this incredible gift. I turned onto his street and saw clusters of townhomes amid huge Douglas fir and cedar trees. They were so big that much of the street was shady. His place was on a corner, with a group of trees in the front yard and another soaring beyond the fence shading his back yard. I looked at the two-story building with its tidy front lawn and pulled into the driveway. As I got out of my car, I heard the wind weaving through the cedar branches, a sound that has always soothed me. Walking up to the door, I grinned when I saw wind chimes and a collection of seashells along the wall—two of my favorite things.

I rang the doorbell, and my dad opened the door. He had the same blue eyes that I remembered, but his dark brown hair was now silver. I had dressed up for this special occasion, wearing a favorite pink skirt and a colorful scarf, with my long hair twisted up on my head.

"You look just like your mother," he said. I didn't know quite how to take that but came to realize that I was just a handful of years older than Mum when she'd left Dad, never to see him again.

After he introduced me to his wife Marlene, there were hugs all around. Then he and I sat in the living room to visit. Over cups of tea we exchanged information about our lives and compared notes on likes, dislikes, and what was most important to us. I continued to feel the pressure of a deep well of emotions just below the surface. There was so much I wanted to share, but it was all tangled up with the dysfunction and abuse of my growing-up family. I felt the importance of taking this reunion slowly, to get to know Dad and let him get to know me. There would be time for the deeper stuff after I felt more comfortable. I asked him questions about his favorite pastimes, favorite foods, books to read, places to travel. There was so much to know and discover.

The sun shone through the trees outside, touching the windows in a few places with glimmering fingers. It was a relaxed, pleasant, and earnest conversation. I found in my father a nature similar to mine—outward facing, compassionate, and tolerant but a little fiery around the edges when we saw unfairness. I'd never found adults in my growing-up family who thought like I did and generally was mocked for my opinions on social justice and compassion.

Dad was completely accepting of me. He didn't question or criticize. He simply wanted to know more and to be in my life. At the age of thirty-one, it was the beginning of finding my true place of belonging.

I'm glad I waited to tell Dad about my childhood. When I eventually did tell him that Frank sexually abused me and shattered my young life, he cried. He still does not know the full extent of what my sister and I had experienced in our childhoods and beyond. We decided it would break his heart.

CHAPTER 40

near misses

During the next few months as we pieced together our histories and met more of each other's friends and Marlene's family, it emerged that Paul and Janie already had multiple existing but undiscovered connections to Dad. Even more surprising, Dad and Marlene had multiple connections to Paul and Janie. No matter how we looked at it, we had to marvel at the near misses and wonder how our paths had not crossed earlier.

The first remarkable coincidence happened the day after Paul and Janie met Dad and Marlene. Paul called his friend who worked at Safeway to thank him for the union office number and to share the fantastic news. The friend was curious about Janie's father's name. When Paul told him, he was "staggered," because he'd known our father for years. The friend was in management, and Dad visited his store regularly as the union representative for the store's employees. They had met over many cups of coffee. He exclaimed to Paul, "Why didn't you ever just tell me the name of Janie's dad? I could have hooked you up a decade ago!"

In the summer of 1986, Paul and Janie hosted a barbeque to introduce Dad and Marlene to all of their friends. Dad and Marlene invited their friends and Marlene's sister and brother-in-law. The party was in full swing on a sunny day in the garden; everyone was enjoying the gathering. One of Janie and Paul's closest friends arrived a bit late and walked into the yard with a case of beer. He had known Paul since high school and recently got his certification as an electrician. He immediately noticed Marlene's brother-in-law, laughed out loud and said, "Hey, what the hell are you doing here?" Paul's close friend and Marlene's brother-in-law, also an electrician, had been working together for two years.

Another time, Janie and Paul were chatting with Dad and discovered a further coincidence from the past. Before they bought a house in Langley, they had owned a condominium in New Westminster. While they lived there, Dad drove past their building every day on his way to and from work.

Then there was the neighborhood near miss. I moved away from Tsawwassen in March 1973. In 1975, Mum and Frank made the decision to move to the Caribbean that changed Janie's life. Meanwhile, Dad had been working for various Safeway stores in Vancouver for a few years by then. His employer sent him out to the Tsawwassen Safeway's meat department in 1974 for two weeks and then for a day or two at a time into 1975. It was not a big town—more of a village—and to get to our house required driving right by that Safeway, one of only two local grocery stores where residents, including my family, stopped for groceries.

Dad was working just blocks from the house where one of his daughters lived, and crossing paths seemed likely. It never happened, and then Janie was gone. So close and yet so far apart.

It was a snow globe full of swirling connections, all within reach.

 part three

CHAPTER 41

grandma's funeral

Sometime in the late 1980s Grandma had a heart attack but survived. Mum blamed the cardiac disaster on my insistence on talking to Grandma about disturbing things. As she aged, Grandma evolved from a dedicated smoker into an occasional puffer, but after her heart attack she quit altogether.

Continuing to wage war on germs, she had a second door to her bathroom installed, a major source of hilarity in the family, at least for those of us still speaking. On the few occasions that a group of family visited her, we never warned newcomers about the original door, which was inside the doorsill mere inches apart from the new, second door. We just waited for the unsuspecting person to open one door and crash into the next one. Paul's first encounter with the doors became part of family lore.

Always a champion walker, once she recovered from the heart attack Grandma continued striding to the beach where she sunned herself on her favorite bench, but sometimes she took the bus downtown with her discount senior pass. It was a huge compromise, but she retained her dignity.

Then around 1989, Grandma had a stroke that immobilized her left side. When she survived that but was disabled, I talked to her about the possibility of having her house remodeled to allow her to live there in a wheelchair, but I was subsequently shouted down by Mum on the phone. She was furious that I had "interfered."

In 1990 Grandma went to live in a nursing home—something she had dreaded all her senior years and had begged me to make sure never happened. However, she had not given me the legal power to ensure her wishes were carried out, so Mum took charge.

I visited Grandma nearly every week, working hard to avoid Mum and especially Frank, who quietly hurled invectives at me in a controlled but nasty voice when he saw me. Grandma lived only a year in the nursing home, and then she was gone.

Despite all of her acrobatics with the truth and her ongoing manipulations, I had loved her and was brokenhearted at her passing.

She had a comfortable estate, and Mum was the executor. The house was paid off and Grandma had investments and savings. In her will she directed that her estate be divided four ways: between her two children—Mum and Uncle Stewart—and between Janie and me. I was grateful for the inheritance and wondered if it was Grandma's way of saying sorry. Mum was emphatically clear that she was not happy about losing part of *her* inheritance to her kids.

Mum invited me over to the Victorian house on the road to the sea to talk about household items that had not been specifically directed to anyone in the will. I knocked on the door; it was startling to see her unfriendly face after all the years of Grandma opening the door and saying, "Hello dahling." Mum walked me to three of Grandma's lesser antiques: a damaged dresser, a chair, and a lamp that didn't work. She said something like, "These are for you if you want them." I asked about Grandma's teacups, which I adored. Not available. I asked about one piece of clothing to remember her by: a shell pink, light wool sweater that always looked great on Grandma. "We'll see," Mum said. I was ushered out the door as I thanked Mum for the three items. The house was subsequently sold.

Mum arranged for an open casket at Grandma's funeral. When I walked up to pay my respects, I saw Grandma's familiar folded hands and then my heart pounded in astonishment as I heard myself gasp. She was wearing the shell pink sweater.

CHAPTER 42

grandpa's broken heart

Grandpa moved to the Victoria area in his declining years after his wife Harriet had died. He had retired and lived a quiet life in an apartment. I began to visit him. He was still tall, but stooped from age, and his hair had thinned to baldness. He seemed gentler, and his health was not great. In the early 1990s a heart attack felled him, but he recovered. He acquired a much younger girlfriend who called me regularly to lecture me about providing for my grandfather financially.

Even though family connections remained important to me, I reluctantly distanced myself from Mum and not at all reluctantly from Frank. I made the decision around 1989 because of their toxic behavior after Dad had come back into my life. On her birthday and on each Mother's Day I would send Mum loving cards and letters explaining that I was willing to work on repairing our relationship with the help of family counseling. She never took me up on the offer, and I was completely done with her emotional and financial bamboozlements. She did, however, remain in touch with Grandpa.

After Grandpa's heart attack, he cried more easily, which at first I found alarming. He'd always had an exceptionally stiff upper lip. I can't remember if I told him about the abuse from Frank, but I do recall that Grandpa never liked him. Of course, Grandpa liked very few people.

During one visit over cups of tea, Grandpa told me he'd received a letter from his cousin in England that greatly concerned him. The cousin had asked about me as to whether I'd received treatment for my mental illness. Apparently during several visits to England in the late 1980s and early 1990s, Mum had informed the family that I was a full-blown psychiatric case. I stared at him, stunned. Grandpa informed me that he wrote back to the cousin to tell her that I was fine, had always been fine, and was a responsible adult with a good career in government.

Then Grandpa revealed that Mum had "borrowed" smallish amounts of money from him over the past few years, always promising to pay him back; but when he asked about repayment, she gave reasons why she couldn't. I'd had similar monetary experiences with her and knew how slick and sly she was about money. Most recently she had secured several thousand from him, his remaining liquid savings, for an "important business investment." He'd finally realized that she was never going to return the money. I came to learn from my sister that Mum had spent the money on a stud dog that she imported from England for breeding.

It turned out that Mum had "borrowed" money from most everyone in the family. Usually, she made a request due to an "impending financial disaster" that required immediate relief, or a "fantastic investment opportunity." Over time, I gave her about $2600, which was quite a bit in the 1980s and early 1990s. When, after waiting patiently for repayment, I asked about her plans to repay me, she would fix me with a look of profound surprise and say, "But I thought it was a gift!" Others also gave "loans," and even our penurious grandmother parted with cash on her behalf.

Grandpa sat on the couch, looked off into the distance, and said that he felt his life had been a failure. I asked, "Is that because of Mum?" He said it was and lowered his head and wept softly. I held his hand and felt a few tears lurking behind my eyes.

He died in 1995 after a second, fatal heart attack. Mum was the executor of his estate, which probably had been very small. She excluded me from all final arrangements, including scattering Grandpa's ashes. I found his obituary in the newspaper, and it remains in a file I have today marked "Family," along with Grandma's obituary, both written by Mum. I reread them recently and wondered how much of the information in them is true.

As I was writing this memoir, my cousin Adrienne found a collection of very old family photos that had been digitized; she sent a link to my sister and me. They were a revelation. There was Grandpa, a young man, slender and tall, smiling at the camera. He had a full head of wavy blonde hair and a hopeful face. I had only ever known him as a bald, overweight, often-cynical patriarch with a seething temper. I don't think he planned to become an angry bully who threatened anyone he did not like or those who had crossed him. At least I hope not. I am sure he did not look at his new baby daughter and say, "I know you are going to break my heart many times and it will turn me into a bitter old man." The old, fading photos helped me to see that he had been a young man with dreams and hopes and plans, just like so many others starting out in life.

CHAPTER 43

you can't argue with cancer

I spent years trying to tame my relationship with my mother. She reminded me a little of a blonde version of the volatile characters played by Elizabeth Taylor. She was glamorous, funny, charming, often polished, sometimes shrewish, unpredictably cruel, unbelievably generous, occasionally imperious, somewhat earthy, had an answer for everything, and had a temper that fell onto the heads of the unsuspecting.

Frequently bedridden with migraines, she had disconcerting mood swings that made for adventurous and sometimes dangerous family times. She knew just how to make me laugh and just how to skewer me into wounded silence with her words. Her presence towered over our family like a pirate ship, full of treasure and terror. The estrangement I chose left me more stable emotionally but removed me from a decade of communication with her.

Mum was diagnosed with cancer in 1998 when she was in her late 60s. She argued with the doctors, would not cooperate with the treatment plan, and generally lived in her own reality as she had always done. This was one circumstance that she could not spin or manipulate or shape to her own version of the truth. As I understand from my sister, she was a very difficult patient.

That was a year of firsts: in the spring of 1998 I married for the first time; in the early summer I had abdominal surgery for the first time to remove a mass that was not cancer; in the fall both my husband and I were diagnosed with cancer. I was told I would likely not survive, and so I decided to reconnect with Mum. She still was a difficult mother and our visits were never long.

Together, but as distant as neighboring galaxies, we battled our particular brands of cancer. She lost a great deal of weight, and I realized what a tiny frame had hosted all that charm, wit, toxicity, and talent. Meanwhile, I was bloated from my medication's side effects and felt like a giant parade balloon next to her.

Surprisingly, I turned out to be a survivor, and my spouse and I moved from Victoria to the US, his home country, seeking the specialized care he needed. He and I held onto a hopeful prognosis, but the cancer in his body raged forward unexpectedly and his zest for life disappeared as tumors pushed through healthy tissue. When the cancer reached his brain, he seesawed from outbursts of wrath and vitriol to risky, childlike behavior that left me exhausted.

After an emergency hospital visit, I arranged for him to be moved to hospice care. He was leaving me at forty-six, far too soon and far too young. I sat by his bedside, my hair just barely covering my scalp after my chemo had released its grip, watching and grieving as he slipped in and out of a coma. On February 18, 2000, his breathing changed, and the nurse said it wouldn't be long. It wasn't. Between sobs I kept telling him it was OK to go, that I would be all right. Later that day he let go, and I fell into a pool of grief.

Eventually cancer overtook my mother like a dark star imploding, and she, too, went into hospice. My sister, ever the faithful caregiver, called me to say that Mum had briefly awakened from a coma on February 19, 2000. That was my sister's birthday, and mine would follow just a few days later. Janie said, "I know you've just had a huge loss, and I didn't want to call. But I think she is waiting for you, and I'm pretty sure she's going to wake up on your birthday like she did on mine. Can you come?" I knew I had to try. My chemo arm throbbed and was hypersensitive to touch. My knees crackled and ached on stairs. But I had to try.

I traveled the eight hours to Victoria, weeping with sadness and exhaustion and frustration. On February 27, my birthday, I arrived at the hospital. I found my sister, and we hugged for a long moment and then walked to the hospice unit. Hospice care was bereft of urgency, lacking the noisy collections of medical machines and rushed feet of nurses. There were just a few rooms in this wing of the small hospital, and they had more color and softness than their cousins, the rooms devoted to sterility and the science of healing. I wondered why color is an outlaw in some hospitals. Then I saw my stepfather, and he stared at me unpleasantly. We walked past him into Mum's room. Frank hovered at the door, glaring.

I saw a very small form in the bed, covered in a pretty quilt. My sister talked to me quietly, explaining that Mum had not awakened since February 19. Then she walked out the door, taking Frank for a "cup of tea." I was transfixed by Mum's head, which was perched on the pillow like a nestling bird, gaunt and outstretched, closed eyelids lined with veins. Her head was at exactly the same angle as my husband's head as he lay dying a few days before. Mouth slightly agape, nose sharp, eye sockets like dark cups, neck straining up and out, hair slick from lying in bed. The sight hurt in ways I was not anticipating.

I settled quietly in the chair next to her bed. Rarely had I seen her without her hair done and at least a bit of makeup. It was as if I was seeing a miniature version of my mother who had slipped free of adornment and was lying pale and unexpectedly silent. Her hair was silver and gray—the first time I'd seen her natural color in thirty years—and it was the same shade as mine. I was uncertain whether to touch her, so I leaned forward and spoke softly, "Hi Mum, I'm here." Her lovely green eyes opened and stared directly into my green eyes, pinning me to my chair. Even through the veil of heavy medication she knew me. Out of instinct, I braced for the flash of her personality, for words to flow, but her speech was garbled. I couldn't make out what she was saying, so instead I stroked her hair, marveling that it felt just exactly like mine.

I had a few words of love and peace; not many. They were pulled away into an ocean of unsettled business. Dwelling in the sadness, I continued to stroke her hair, smiling softly at her. Impossibly, I hoped she would apologize to me—for something, for anything in my childhood. It was a wild desire for a death-bed reconciliation, a moment of tears and forgiveness. But her eyelids finally closed firmly, hiding the emerald spheres that had looked at me in so many ways through the years, and I knew she was gone into another place beyond my reach. There would never be any shared words of grace or gratitude, any last wish whispered, any joy over a life well lived. I was deeply grateful for the medication that kept her detached from her decimated body. Her breathing was unhurried—softer and slower, so unlike the powerful energy I knew during her life.

I knew she was fully in the shadow of death, and I also knew I could not sit through another life ending so close to my husband's. I could not hold her hand as I did his, weeping over his beautiful fingers that were untouched by disease, looking as though they could still glide over piano keys and play his beloved gospel songs. I could not labor by her bedside as I did with my husband, watching his breathing stop and then lurch into a gasp, his head moving into that peculiar posture of the dying, reaching upward for the next gulp of air. I could not lie across her bed as I did his, desperate for the gulps and gasps to stop, urging him to let go, and finally feel that last breath tearing my heart. And I certainly could not sit in the same room as my stepfather, under his hateful stare, watching my mother's last moments. So I left. I went to stay with a friend. I clung to my shredded faith and waited, breathing two words heavenward:

Help me—help me—help me.

The next day, February 28, she was gone, flitting out of her wounded body. When my sister called and told me, it was like air leaving my lungs and filling them at the same time. Grief and relief became an odd couple struggling inside my body. My soul felt like cement. I stayed to help with the arrangements for her memorial, knowing I would go home to make another set of arrangements for my husband's memorial. A few days later at her service, when it came time for family to speak, I paid tribute to her strength and her creativity as I looked at the grieving faces of a roomful of her friends. I wondered what they would think if they knew the true story of her life and reluctantly decided they would not believe me.

The Quest

I returned and returned to you,
trying to make you,
mold you,
press you
into the shape of love.

I did not grasp
that you could not,
would not
because your jaws
were already full.

I gentled you in
my daydreams, but
only death could
quiet your ravenous grip
and stop the pain.

I carry my sorrow
across your memory
as I unfurl my wings
to lift and soar
away from your shadow.

CHAPTER 44

a bitter tapestry

During the time she was in hospice, I had not known that when Mum woke up on February 19 she was coherent. Janie had been sitting by her bed, quietly keeping vigil, not expecting to have a conversation.

My husband did the same thing. He had been in a light coma for a few days, then woke up, ate a meal, and talked to several of us in the room. Our conversation was lighthearted and sweet, for which I was thankful. Later in the day, he lay back down, never to awaken again. The hospice nurse told me patients would sometimes wake up for a few hours before falling into a deep coma.

I suppose my sister did not tell me what Mum said when she briefly woke up because I was already distraught about my double loss only days apart. A year or two after Mum died, Janie opened up. She'd been at Mum's bedside for days, watching as she slept more and more deeply. On February 19 when Mum opened her eyes, Janie leaned in and said, "Hi Mum," and smiled. She spoke softly, saying that it was OK for Mum to go, and she promised to stay by her side so she'd never be alone.

Mum turned her head toward Janie and responded, "I hate you. I have always hated you and I don't want you here! I want Angela."

Janie had jerked back in her chair, stunned and heartbroken. She gathered herself and replied quietly, "Well, that's too bad Mum. I promised you from the start I'd stay with you, and I will not break that promise." As her fire burned down to its last embers, Mum slipped fully into a coma.

When I first received this information, I simply did not know what to do with it. It was so hard to digest that I placed it in a corner of my mind, and it slipped into its own dark place of forgetfulness. Then Janie reminded me of it as she was reading a first draft of this story, and the cheerless coal of memory flared into life again. At first, I was moved by my sister's strength and kindness in keeping that bitter and divisive retort out of my last moments with Mum. Then a bewildering flow of questions filled my mind. Why would a dying mother say such a thing to her own child? Especially when that daughter had been consistently kind and considerate toward her? Why did she favor me, the one who did not want her company? Had the high doses of morphine affected her thinking?

I thought back a couple of decades. When my sister and I became adults, Mum developed a malicious tactic. She threw emotional bombs between us, made of twisted half-truths and bald-faced lies designed to keep us at odds with each other. I don't know why; perhaps she got some kind of warped reward out of manipulating our sibling relationship. The stories of parents or guardians controlling children and the consequences of those manipulations are not surprising or new. One manifestation of this is choosing favorites. It is always deeply malicious when parents play siblings against each other like so many chess pieces.

The romantic in me wants to believe that perhaps it was the only way she knew how to express her craving for our love.

I consider it a tragedy that when Grandma died, a measure of calm appeared in our lives. And when Mum died, a noticeable tranquility settled over us. My relationship with my sister began to heal. As our mother's tapestry of lies unraveled and the truth appeared, our trust in each other grew. It took several years, but we did it.

Mum's death also revealed that Frank had the beginnings of dementia. Janie and Paul visited him regularly at the home he'd shared with Mum. True to their pattern of several decades, Mum and Frank had lost their farm. They quietly moved to a mobile home. Mum put out a flower stand and planted a garden, keeping the place as nice as she could, but it was a big step down. They joined the local Rotary, and she became a rising star in that membership. Then she suddenly closed her flower shop. They kept going to Rotary until she got too sick to drive. Frank was left alone in the small, nicely-decorated home he'd shared with Mum, facing a pile of debts that she had incurred in both their names.

It wasn't long before Frank's behaviors became concerning to Janie and Paul. Nearly 80, he still worked hauling trailer loads of junk to the dump for customers. Sometimes he'd forget to take the junk to the dump and just unload it at home. From time to time, he called Janie to say he didn't know where he was or how to get home. By then, Janie and Paul were living on Salt Spring Island, and getting to Frank's house required a ferry ride—she couldn't just hop in the car and find him. Still, she did her best to guide him home. I was living in Portland, Oregon, recovering from my cancer treatment and the financial devastation caused by my illness as well as my late husband's illness and death.

By the end of 2001 and into 2002, when Janie and Paul came to see Frank, they would keep an eye on important keepsakes, and when something was missing from its longtime spot, Paul would distract Frank and Janie would search. She found a glass jar full of watches in the bottom of the washing machine and other times found pizza there. Frank put all of Mum's good china in a broken-down shed with his garden equipment. He gave away quite a few items to sketchy people he would invite over to drink beer; Janie and Paul would sometimes run into them when they visited. Other things were likely stolen. To save a few keepsakes, Janie started asking to "borrow" some china, crystal or other items, and Frank would always say, "Sure, but you have to bring it back." She promised, he forgot, and that's why we have a few mementoes.

Frank stopped showering and often they'd find him sitting in an armchair in his underwear, very drunk and grubby. He appeared to be living on pizza and ice cream. Janie had him evaluated by a cognitive psychologist and had his driver's license revoked because he'd drive off and disappear for days and then show up covered in dirt, unable to remember where he'd been. She and Paul took the keys to his pickup, but Frank somehow produced more keys. When they managed to stop him from driving his truck, he bought a moped.

Janie and Paul went to see Frank's doctor to express their concerns and were astounded by his response. The doctor was curt with them and would not entertain any information they wanted to share, saying they were lying. This was the same doctor who approved the psychological evaluation to cancel Frank's driving license. Mum and Frank had been members of the same Rotary Club as this physician for about five years before Mum died. Together, Mum and Frank had managed to convince everyone there that they lived in a high-end neighborhood and were semi-retired, successful business people. I have no doubt that Frank fed the doctor's mistrust of Janie and Paul and continued to convince the doctor he could live alone.

Janie decided to keep trying and called the doctor to report an injury whenever Frank fell due to being drunk, which was most of the time. The physician responded by asking why she and her husband were slandering Frank's good name. Frank sustained two serious injuries requiring emergency department care, but still this doctor would not believe Janie. Frustrated, Janie and Paul nicknamed Frank's doctor The Pompous Ass. They tracked Frank's behavior and tried to keep him safe. They were puzzled when Frank kept digging around in the garden but decided it was at least a safe pastime.

The situation spiraled to new depths. Frank gave his debit card to a neighbor who promptly stole $1700 from him. Janie got the police involved, but Frank couldn't identify the neighbor, so the police could not pursue the case. On one visit, they found rats running through the small house, and when Janie checked the cupboards and drawers, anything organic or chewable—including the family photo albums, birth certificates, passports and other papers—was gnawed to pieces. There was no paper left in the house, and rats were nesting in the walls.

Janie and Paul persisted with the doctor, who rebuffed their efforts. This went on for two more horrible years. Finally, when the doctor was outright rude to Janie, she was so exhausted and stressed by the whole situation that she put her head on his desk and wept openly. The startled doctor stared at her, and then he said "All right, we'll get to the bottom of this. I'm taking a lunch break and will follow you to Frank's house."

Janie and Paul drove to Frank's place, the doctor behind them in his red Mercedes with white leather upholstery, stepping out into the yard in his expensive tasseled loafers. The yard was a mess, populated with junk.

"Why have you brought me here?" the doctor demanded.

"This is Frank's house," Paul replied.

The doctor stared. As they reached the front steps, they saw two dead rats on the stairs. They opened the front door and invited the doctor to go in first, watching him gingerly step over the rats. The stench stopped him cold. After he gagged, he continued inside, and there were Frank and his brother Walter, in their underwear, roaring drunk, and feeding rats on the kitchen table. Frank looked up, said "Hello doc!" and offered up a beer.

The doctor backed up quickly, told Janie and Frank he'd seen enough, and asked them to come to his office the next day to get the paperwork to have Frank placed in a locked-memory facility. He fairly flew down the stairs to his car. Within two weeks, Frank was moved to a safe, secure, clean facility on Salt Spring Island near Janie and Paul. The Pompous Ass had allowed Frank to run feral for three years, blocking all of Janie's efforts to get him into a secure setting and leaving a wrecked house and yard for Janie and Paul to clean up.

Frank's conniving days were over when in 2004 he was moved to the facility where he would live for a decade until his death. He spent his days walking the halls singing, visiting with other residents and talking to staff. When Janie and Paul were cleaning out what was left in the mobile home, she decided to collect some of the roses in the garden that Mum had planted. Paul dug up a few plants, then his shovel clanked on metal: he had found the metal cremation urn with Mum's remains. Frank had been burying it, digging it up, and reburying it around the garden.

Janie stopped visiting when Frank no longer remembered her, a couple of years into his time at the memory-care unit. As Frank continued on his journey into oblivion, still more peace came into our small extended family. When he died in 2014, I felt sorrow for the choices he had made that wounded us so profoundly, but mostly I was relieved. Finally, Janie was completely free of his bitter burden, and she and I could bloom together.

CHAPTER 45

fire follower

My mother's death sometimes left me completely numb, while at other times I contended with a stream of memories that would pop up without notice.

"You!" My mother's words smacked at my weeping teenage face, "I am *sick* and *tired* of your crying. Why do you always have to under*stand* and *care* about everything?" It was yet another argument about a since-forgotten topic that started with me asking a question and ended with me unable to talk because she had detoured around the truth by ridiculing my need to understand. As I stood before the memory of her sneer, I wondered about my time in her womb. When I shifted my baby weight, what did she think? Did she say nasty things?

I remembered her grabbing my ten-year-old hands and dancing me around the kitchen, giggling and making funny faces as we swayed to the waves of her favorite surf band on the turntable, tossing this way and that. The power of her beauty and teasing splashed across my young heart, and I wanted to twist and shout and follow my wildfire mother.

I thought about her father flying through Luftwaffe gunfire over WW II Britain, surviving with the few, only to later make his family mark with generous spending and equally liberal doses of his bad temper.

I wondered how I could so resemble Grandpa's daughter that at my second wedding her surviving family and sturdier friends gasped in astonishment—and perhaps fear—as I walked down the aisle into my new life. How my laughter floated through that blazing hot summer day, a ghost of hers, lacking the glittering, sharp edges.

I wondered about her swirling currents of DNA in my form. How I could have her green eyes, her smile, her gestures, her laugh, and yet be stymied by so much guilt, along with compassion and regret? She had been unfettered by such chemistry of attachment, pushing her own world forward, certain that she deserved everything she desired, joking or raging like sudden weather.

I wondered if she knew she had burned down her own dreams or that her children would plant beauty in her wake, rising like lupines out of the gray and the dead.

CHAPTER 46

ashes

After Mum was cremated, Frank got the ashes. As his dementia progressed from 2000 to 2004, many things in the home that he and Mum shared were misplaced, broken, or went missing. When Paul found Mum's ashes in the garden, Janie took the urn back to their house. She kept the ashes for a few years and then in 2010, she was ready to scatter them on Salt Spring Island. Frank was lost to dementia by about 2006, so Janie was able to make the decision without involving him. This is what she wrote to me and a couple of other family members about the event.[1]

> I laid my mother to rest today. I did not wake up this morning and say "Today's the day!" No, I was cleaning out the fridge when I got the overwhelming urge to go outside. Weird I know, but there it is. It was the most beautiful day, the colors so crisp and the air clean with the smell of autumn . . .
> It was time.

I had been looking at family photos of years gone by, and I realized that my mother was the happiest when she was by the ocean, sitting on a rock while the ocean breezes drifted past her face and the sun warmed her. I drove through the falling leaves to Ruckle Park and marveled at the trees, so lovely in their yellows, golds, and reds, and knew I was making the right decision to lay Mom's ashes to rest in the ocean where she spent happy times.

I know a few of you had said you wanted to be present when the time came, but I hope you'll understand that this was a journey I had to take alone. My mother had spent too much time in a metal box, and it was my right to set her free and finally say the things that needed saying out loud. I forgave my mom, or I thought I had, a long time ago for the things she did, the things she said, and the things she didn't say. But today as I stood in the bright fall sunshine, I realized I had been waiting for this moment to really let it all out. So, I said it out loud for the birds, crickets, bees, the ocean—anything or anybody within hearing distance.

    I forgive you mom, for hitting me.
    I forgive you mom, for kicking me.
    I forgive you mom, for leaving me.
    I forgive you mom, for coming back to us when you didn't want to.
    I forgive you mom, for not looking after me properly.
    I forgive you mom, for taking me away from my father.

I forgive you mom, for not loving me.

I forgive you mom, for not wanting me.

That day I forgave my mom a LOT of things. But I also thanked my mother for having me. Thanked my mother for my sister. I thanked my mother for the abuse because it made me stronger! It gave me the strength to raise my two beautiful children to be loving, strong, kind, and independent. Something they can pass on to their children, which they are doing now. The abuse stopped with me because, unlike my mother, I wanted children, and I love my children so much it hurts, and thank God every day I had the strength to survive. Most don't! No one should be thankful for abuse . . . at any time. What a thing to be thankful for!! But I am.

As I stood in the bright fall sunshine at the park looking into the clear water, listening to Ave Maria by Il Divo and watching the waves lap up the earthly remains of my mother, I was very sad that she spent most of her life unhappy and unfulfilled. There was so much to be thankful for! I know she did have some wonderful times when she could forget the past, but it always crept back when she wasn't looking. You can't escape your past; you can only accept it and move on, something Mom could not do, even at the very end of her life.

As her journey came to an end, I hope she found peace at last.

Janie's letter was riveting. I read it a few times, cried, and reflected on her decision. At first I was troubled that Janie had scattered Mum's ashes without me, but I decided she deserved the choice because she'd cared for Mum at the end and endured her spite and hate. I put the letter away.

A few years on, I finally saw that Mum was far more abusive to Janie. The heavy weight that Janie carried was painful, personal, and heart-rending. She had to say goodbye alone.

CHAPTER 47

disappointments

In 2009, Uncle Stewart—our mother's brother—emailed my sister and me to share a collection of family photos he'd made and was digitizing. We both wrote back asking for a copy. I explained that Mum had discarded most of the pictures taken during our early childhood, while Janie wrote that most of those that had been left had been destroyed after Mum's death due to Frank's dementia. Uncle Stewart's response included some interesting and unexpected comments.

> Dec. 18. 2009
>
> Of course, you will get everything that I have of you and the family. The loss of photos is so tragic and I don't understand Rose destroying her own family history—there were wonderful pictures of you and Janie, your mother and Al. The whole situation was bizarre in my estimation, and I can only assume she was somewhat depressed.

> I don't have many pictures of you after the very emotional breakdown of your parents' marriage because I didn't see much of you, as you moved west and I left home to start university. I was completely devastated by the turn of events, the same as your grandparents. I don't think mother [he always called Grandma "mother"] ever got over the shock of it all and subsequent events.
> I'm so happy for you now that everything is so good in your life ... I'm sure that if you'd had a stable family life when you were growing up that you would have completed university very easily.

Calling our mother "somewhat depressed" was vastly understated. Writing off her misdeeds as the result of slight depression was an excuse. I was very fond of my uncle but also saddened by the possibility that he could have had a destructive role in our young lives. My frustration is that I can't confirm my suspicions, and I don't want to accuse him unfairly. He was twenty-two at the time my sister and I were abducted and easily could have driven the car that took us from our father in 1959.

In 2014, Uncle Stewart and his wife Dani came west for a visit, and it was a pleasant time, though I noticed that he did not look well. At that point, I did not think to ask him about our "move west" as he put it in his email. Later that year we learned that he had been diagnosed with abdominal lymphoma, stage one, with a good prognosis. To his disappointment, after fifteen months of chemo, the tumor would not relent. By August 2015, he was in congestive heart failure due to damage from the chemo. In September, Dani emailed to say he'd been admitted to hospice, was pain free, and would love to hear from family.

I wrote and said how happy I was that we'd all had time together recently and that I was grateful for his wonderful photography. Perhaps to reassure him—and myself—I said, "While the early years were not easy, I want you to know that overall, life has been good to me and very rewarding from my late forties onward." Education was always important to him—he had enjoyed a long career as a teacher—and I told him I was closer to getting my degree. My closing wished him only peace and blessings as he entered hospice. He responded to my letter with sincerity.

> Sept. 11, 2015
>
> Dear Angela: Thank you so much for your lovely, supportive email. I'm lying in bed in hospital having just received the news that there is no further treatment for me, and I will go to palliative care at another hospital or hospice. I'm in no pain at the moment, but I'm told there will be in the future.
>
> Thank goodness we met recently in BC—it was so wonderful to see you all again. I treasure the memory.
>
> I know you had such a rough time as a child, and I used to listen to frantic worries about your upbringing. Grandma/pa were worried excessively about you both all the time. I dreaded reading Grandma's letters because they were so depressing and there was nothing I could do about the situation. I just couldn't understand my sister's bizarre behavior! 5,000 km of geographic separation and no money made for an impossible situation.
>
> (I just had a shot for pain and it makes me sleepy.)

I'm so pleased that you both have been able to adjust and overcome your childhood difficulties and painful memories. It hasn't been easy for you.

Congratulations on your academic progress—if you'd had a normal childhood, you would have finished your education with the rest of students your age. So sad you missed out on this. You are doing so well now academically—keep up the good work—I am really proud of you.

Love,
Uncle S

Nine days later, I received an email from Dani with a newspaper clipping attached.

Obituary

Peacefully, on September 20, 2015, in St. Catharine's Hospital. In his seventy-eighth year. Beloved husband . . . father . . . stepfather . . . grandpa . . . uncle.

Stewart was born in Canterbury, England and lived four years in Egypt before his family emigrated to Toronto in 1952. Stewart graduated from the University of Toronto in Economics and taught economics in Scarborough. He loved photography, investing, RVing, traveling, and soccer . . . . Missed but never forgotten.

A reader would never be able to guess from his letter that Uncle Stewart might have played a part in separating us from our father. And perhaps he didn't. There are two reasons I placed him on that trip. My clear memory is that he scooped me up from the water's edge when I was four and nearly drowned at the beach. My grandmother confirmed my memory of the wave, and although I don't recall whether she mentioned Uncle Stewart, I've been writing about that experience with him in it since my early thirties. Additionally, it seemed odd to me that Grandpa could have driven the car that took us across the US in 1959 and also could have been in Oakville to organize packing and moving his household across the country, to take Dad's call about us girls coming home, and then come over to Dad's house and remove almost all its contents.

Uncle Stewart could have been a genuine observer as his letters indicate, worrying from a distance about his two nieces. Maybe he wasn't. Certainly, he grew up in a family that had no scruples about lying with great sincerity whenever it suited them. Now it's too late to know. This kind of doubt becomes a persistent dilemma for survivors of childhood abuse. That is why I went to significant lengths to corroborate events in our younger years whenever I could, and why I could not say with confidence that Uncle Stewart was directly engaged in separating us from our father.

He was the last of my mother's immediate family, and he sounded oblivious to what really happened to us, other than referring to the "very emotional breakdown of your parents' marriage," and our mother's "bizarre behavior." He seemed truly sad about the consequences of our mostly terrible childhoods, but like my grandparents, he minimized the wretched behavior of our mother. I, too, am sad that I have cause to suspect him of having a role in our suffering.

CHAPTER 48

dental requiem

Throughout my adult years, I've had a great deal of dental work done to repair an asymmetrical jaw and crooked teeth. When I was in my late twenties, my jaw drove me to a specialist—it clicked and popped and crackled and never opened or closed properly. The surgeon took an X-ray and showed me the problem. "Your right jaw was broken at some early point in your life and didn't heal properly. It doesn't fit in the socket. Do you remember when it was broken?" I stared at him, surprised, and told him I had no memory of a broken jaw.

In subsequent years of repair work performed in other dental offices, more dentists looked at their imaging and said the same thing to me, and I gave them the same answer. Each one would say something to the effect of, "Well, it looks exactly like an old break that healed badly."

Eventually, in my early thirties I chose to have jaw surgery to correct the malfunction, mostly because the procedure was presented as a lifetime solution. In preparation for the surgery, I wore braces for a year and a half, and after the surgery, I wore them for another six months. During the operation, my jaw was broken and realigned and fastened into its new shape with titanium plates. However, my jaw did not heal as expected after the surgery, and it was wired shut for six weeks. When everything finally healed and the braces came off, I was thrilled.

Fifteen years later, my teeth had partially reverted to their previous crooked ways, and I noticed my jaw was losing its stability. A new dentist informed me that the earlier procedure I'd had was, at the time, thought to be a permanent cure, but since then dentists had come to realize that it was not. I needed further treatment. More X-rays and more questions about my weirdly shaped right jaw. "When did you break it as a child?"

Each time a dentist said this, I delved into my memory. What I slowly came to realize is that no one ever *told* me I had a broken jaw as a child.

Yet another dentist, an older man, told me he was quite sure the anomaly in my right jaw was a healed break. By then I'd come to terms with the violence of my childhood, and I explained to him that I didn't remember it being broken, but I'd been hit often as a youngster, and perhaps one of those incidents was the cause. He took my hand in his and very gently said, "I'm so sorry that happened to you. Today, we'd be sure to report such a crime, and you'd have been protected." He surprised me by calling my injury a crime, by his compassionate response, and by his vigilance for the safety of children. I wished someone like him had been in my life when I was young. Unfortunately, I don't share his confidence about the safety of abused children today.

After that appointment, I asked Dad if he remembered me ever having a broken jaw while he was a part of the first four years of my life. "Nope, never," he said. During the next few months, two memories emerged.

In the earliest memory, I was about seven and living with my mother, my sister, and my mother's boyfriend Kurt in Victoria, BC. Mum's dreadful migraines resulted in violent vomiting, weeping, moaning, and general misery for the entire household. The whole experience made me shaky with alarm. One day she came out of the bathroom, staggered down the hall clutching her head and gave me a $5 bill, telling me to go to the store and get her migraine medicine. "Be sure to get the small size because that's all the money I have, and I need the change."

I took off at a run. At the store, I found only the larger size. I wanted her to be better so after some hesitation, I bought it. She met me inside the front door. I handed her the pills and a bit of change and started to explain. She shouted, "You did what I told you not to do!" and shoved me backwards and I almost fell. Then she began to scream at me and backhanded the right side of my face, full force. The back of my head slammed into the floor first and my lungs emptied. She was still screaming. She might have kicked me—the memory fades out at this point.

In the later memory I was a teenager in the dentist's chair. We were living in Tsawwassen around 1970, and I was having my wisdom teeth removed to make room for my other teeth, in hopes they would straighten. I was numbed and also given gas to help me relax, and I promptly went to sleep. I remember briefly waking from my drugged daze, seeing the dentist brace himself on my chair arm and hearing a crunching sound from my lower jaw. Then I fell asleep again. When I fully woke up the next day, my face was hugely swollen and deeply bruised. My sister recently reminded me that I missed a lot of school because healing took several weeks. She feels the dentist absolutely could have broken my jaw. I wondered whether it had been broken earlier and then re-fractured by the extraction.

At a dental appointment in my fifties, after going through a second set of two-year braces and years of dental splint therapy to help my bite alignment, I recounted the wisdom-teeth-extraction memory and asked the dentist if that might have broken my jaw. He had also seen the X-ray. "Doubtful," he said, "you would have been younger."

I have pored through photos of me as a toddler through my teens. I noticed that there is a slight asymmetry to my jaw as early as age three; however, it became much more pronounced after the traumatic removal of my wisdom teeth in my teenage years. Was my jaw broken at birth? Before I walked? When I was two? Why didn't Dad know about it? Was it fractured again in my teens?

There are no answers, no confessions, no proof. The doubt haunts me every time I have another dental procedure to try and stabilize my jaw.

CHAPTER 49

the nightmare speaks

Those two terrified young girls walking down dark stairs in my early nightmare were real, even though the strange prison-like castle and the booming, menacing voice were not. Even now I feel a resurging sense of horror when I focus on the memory of that dream—my desperate feeling of being pulled down, down, down while being mocked by a ghastly male voice. The awful reality was that we truly were alone with a series of abusers. As a young girl, I couldn't understand or cope with the amount of fear I felt in my waking hours, so the fear came out in my dreams.

Being a lifelong worrier in perpetual recovery, I believe that nightmares manifest unarticulated worries and fears and dark truths. Those things that we cannot speak, that reside in the unseen caverns of our unconscious, in my case were buried there since early childhood. If my young self could have spoken her nightmare into words, this is what she might have voiced:

We are lost.
It is not safe.
There is no one to help us.
I can't reach my sister.
She is in danger.
Once she is gone, I am alone.
I am in danger.
I am so afraid.

When I thought about the nightmare in my past years, I had some firm assumptions. I saw it as an older-sibling guilt dream about not being able to protect my sister from harm in an abusive family. While neither my sister nor I were perfect children, our antics and squabbles were met by outsized and out-of-control responses. As the big sister, I saw her as tiny and doll-like, so fragile when she was being verbally or physically abused. I was older and bigger and able, so I thought, to intervene and did not. I was fearful, especially of being struck. I still carry the weight of that guilt, and continue to work through it. However, as I have excavated the memory of that nightmare in this memoir, I have found other meanings.

The dream seems to indicate that even as a young girl, I understood that we were not going to be rescued from danger, which could have been why it recurred. At some point in my childhood, I would have realized that my kind and patient father was gone—forever. And, when bad stuff happened at home, it was rarely ever spoken of again and never outside the home. We learned not to talk about what Mum or her boyfriends did to us because she always managed to find out, and we paid the price once she got us alone. When my awareness and understanding of our situation grew, I figured that speaking up might result in my sister and I being separated, which would have been emotionally catastrophic. Somehow, I thought that we were safer together.

Reflecting back, it was remarkably prescient of my young self to recognize through the dream that my sister was very much in danger; even more danger than me. The dream foretold what was to come for her (the most sinister of which I didn't know until I wrote this book). It is a miracle that we both survived, and I thank our guardian angels.

The one constant Janie and I had in our unpredictable young lives was each other. As a girl, the thought of losing Janie must have fed my unspoken fears of being alone. Being the big sister, laden with shame and regret, the idea of me being supported by my little sister had never been part of my understanding. But she truly was a large part of my sense of safety. Even though it has come to light through a nightmare, it is a beautiful realization for my life today. We were each other's only constant and reliable family unit until I was eighteen and Janie sixteen. We weathered it all as sisters and got through some really tough times. We didn't talk about it much then, but together we were each other's security.

Finally, the nightmare taught me that most of the monsters in our lives are people pretending to be ordinary.

Now the shouting, angry, wickedly laughing men and women are gone, along with their enablers. Now as adults we are safe, flourishing, and healing together.

CHAPTER 50

unrequited love

When Dad and I talked in 2018 about our 1959 abduction, he said, "Your grandfather was a cruel man. He phoned me once; I think it was just before he died. Out of the blue. He said, 'The girls might have found you, but I'm going to come and kill you!'"

I put timelines together and realized that Grandpa must have made that call during the time he lived in Victoria when I was visiting him, having solicitous cups of tea and holding his hand as he cried. While Grandpa wept over his own failures, he never apologized to me for his part in the devastation of my childhood, and he never gave me a clue that he still had such an entrenched hatred for our father. Based on my conversations with Dad, I realized that over the years Mum likely continued feeding Grandpa's ready rage with fabrications about Dad.

Though Grandma had also spoken of her own failures without the shedding of tears, she never apologized for her continual interference in my young life that brought only sorrow and wreckage. Clearly, Mum had a strong role in shaping Grandma's view of our father, especially if she was the second voice of pivotal false testimony in the court decision to keep him away from my sister and me.

Rooting through the family photos my cousin sent, I saw my grandmother as a young adult, gathered with her large brood of siblings and her parents at a park, probably in London, England, where they had lived. In one image she was in a group of five people, looking so pleasant and lovely as to be unrecognizable to me, except that her distinctive handwriting on the back says, "Happy group taken on Mr. & Mrs. Wheeler's lawn after the garden party, June 1924, after the police cricket match. Me third from left." On the back of another large group photo from that day she wrote, "After the garden party with wives of London City Police, where I met Bert & he became my boyfriend (one of many)." On the front, I saw a small, helpful X made in pen under her chin, just in case there was any doubt.

I find a portrait photo of my grandmother taken on October 10, 1940—one year after the start of World War II. She looks elegant but very sad. By then she was married to my grandfather and had her two children. On the back she wrote, "Reading [a town west of London] suffering broken heart." Someone or something had caused her deep pain. Photos taken that same year of my grandfather show him in uniform standing at the English seaside and then, at a later time, with another officer in Japan. There are photos made of postcards that my grandfather must have sent from Japan, but there is no copy of the backs of the postcards. Snippets of life stories. Much left unsaid.

Among the photos was a print of my mother on one side of Grandma and her brother Stewart on the other. It is a

From left: Stewart, Florence, and Rose, 1944

cheery family snapshot with Mum in her teens and my uncle about nine or ten. For once, Grandma did not write the story on the back, but it was likely during the later years of World War II or just after. The kids were beaming their smiles at the camera, and I noticed Mum was holding her hands the way I often do for photos. Her pose was fetching in a relaxed way, leaning forward slightly, away from her mother and toward her future. Grandma looked considerably older than she did in the earlier photos of her with Bert-One-of-Many, and her smile held hints of the worry that was to become her trademark.

I stared hard at the photos. This family seemed so ordinary, so hopeful, and full of the possibilities of life. Part of my DNA comes from them. Those happy faces were pivotal in removing my father from my life. Before I had all of the truth to answer the many questions about my early childhood, I loved them. When my father was finally back in my life and major parts of the story were revealed, I was angry, but I loved them. I wrestled my way to forgiveness. When I estranged myself from my mother, I did not stop loving her. I missed her as only a daughter can miss her mother.

When I learned the rest of the truth about our abduction while writing this story, I became angry, and my heart broke again, because this family was mine. They are part of my history, my genetics. They gave me my smile, the way I hold my hands, how I lean forward slightly and tilt my head for photos.

I am left with the love. What to do with the love for all of the people involved in shattering our childhood? They were sometimes caring and charming, almost always manipulative, frequently cruel and perverse, generally selfish, insulated by indifference and justification, profoundly dysfunctional, and even sometimes hilarious. My toddler heart loved them all and wanted to be loved back. Children's brains aren't wired to accept that a parent is incapable of loving them. Or that family will love them in ways that wound.

A child's unrequited love doesn't disappear. Over the years it just becomes homeless.

And yet, life is sometimes good enough to rehome a heart.

CHAPTER 51

growing roots

dad has brought hope and a constant positive presence into my life. We always have talked about our dreams for the future and could never have anticipated how many years we would relish together.

Family experiences have abounded. Over the years, there have been countless visits, plenty of friends to meet, and a horde of Marlene's family to know and enjoy at the many dinners and parties Dad and Marlene hosted.

There was a trip to England that Dad and I took in the early 1990s to attend a cousin's wedding, during which my father was able to reconnect with some of his siblings, nieces, and nephews—my aunties, uncles, and cousins—after many years apart. Everywhere in the family I saw people who looked like Janie; it was, and is, wonderful. I had the stuffing hugged out of me and heard stories of how much our aunties loved us when we were tiny and Mum brought us to England for a visit.

There was gradual but tremendous healing for me, especially in my relationship with my sister and Paul after Mum died in 2000. She continued to have an impact on my life with the poisonous words she inexplicably and persistently dripped into family relationships, even though I remained mostly estranged from her until the illness at the end of her life. After she was gone, one overarching reality emerged: Without her presence, a sense of calm settled on the family, and we grew closer and happier.

Since then, I've had some failures, falling back into old emotional patterns, losing friends due to my own dysfunction, but by facing my flaws, I continue to make progress. It's a lifetime of work, and I'll never be finished.

In the years that have followed, I moved on from the little Pentecostal church and its set of cut and dried rules, which eventually constrained me and led to my chafing against the structure and culture of the organization. Happily, I've found other spiritual communities where I can continue exploring the holy mystery that encompasses my understanding and love of God.

Janie and Paul raised their children on Salt Spring. After I was widowed in 2000, I lived and worked in Portland, Oregon, and then was blessed to marry again in 2008. I later transferred with my employer to the Seattle area in Washington state, then my husband Patrick and I retired in Olympia, Washington. Janie and Paul now live in Victoria, BC, as do their two adult children, four grandchildren, and great-grandchildren.

My sister completely broke out of her quiet childhood shell and is outgoing, funny, charismatic, and not afraid of much. She knows just how to make me laugh until I cry, and I'm pretty good at causing her to dissolve into giggles. We both suffer from anxiety but have learned how to cope. We plan what we've dubbed "epic sister trips," just the two of us, to places that interest us.

GROWING ROOTS

Dad and Marlene traveled the world, going to many countries and spending months in some of them, including Australia, where he reconnected with one of his sisters and her family. He and Marlene went to England several times to spend time with the British branch of the family. Back home in Canada, they often took long trips in their RV, heading cross-country or exploring the vastness of their home province of BC.

In 2010, we took a family trip to Hawaii. Paul and Janie, Dad and Marlene, along with Patrick and me, spent ten glorious days on the Big Island. Humpback whales swam right into the inlet where we were staying. We bought avocados the size of grapefruit at the farmer's market. We younger four snorkeled the vivid waters while Dad and Marlene lollygagged on the beach, contending with a pet donkey who roamed the area determined to raid picnic tables, pockets, and bags for snacks. We drove to Volcanoes National Park and saw a vista that no longer exists, consumed by eruptions in 2018. We swam next to green sea turtles that appeared at cleaning stations to be groomed by collections of flashing gold Tang fish and then disappeared into the waves. Dad still talks about that trip, and we all smile and say, "Trip of a lifetime."

Dad, Janie, and I have now been together longer than we were apart. We have our own lived history, rich and full of memories. When he reached ninety, Dad's ongoing health issues kept him closer to home. We have spent plenty of time together since then, supporting him and Marlene when they need our help. Even when the COVID-19 pandemic brought an unwelcome nineteen-month separation with the US-Canada border closed, we relied on our deep mutual affection, our humor, and our

From left: Janie, Al, and Angela in Hawaii, 2010

gratitude to maintain our family connections. As Paul has said, we are a loving, cohesive family. We've got roots, and they are deep.

Now, in 2024, I'm chatting with Dad and Marlene on the phone, talking about our amazing story. "Hasn't it been the best time, Dad?" My voice is just under a shout to be sure he hears me, as his hearing aids need replacement.

His response says it the best. "My life since being back together with you and your sister has been a wonder."

Family Tree

Her face, the gaze so like my father's
that I feel a pang.
Her sturdy spirit pushes against
her unreliable body and sputtering memory.
We smile around the room,
genetics pull us close as we count the years
and treasure the minutes.
How is Auntie Pam, we ask?
How is your father, they ask?
Auntie, uncle, nieces, cousins
sharing jokes and cups of tea
and stories of good days and
surgeries and babies and weather
and all the bits and pieces of life
that knit our twigs and branches
into a multi-country canopy.
He's a darling little pork chop, we say of
the newest baby, all smiles and cowlicks.
He's able to travel again, we say of
our aged father, rallying his body for the trip
to see and hold that baby, his great-great grandson.
We talk about blue eyes and green,
and the names of generations gone,
and how mother and daughter were
buried together because they were never apart in life
and it seemed right.
And yes, we will go and visit the place
where they lay in their forever embrace
while we are in England gathering up
and tending to our roots.

CHAPTER 52

redemption

In the mid-1970s, my sister and I were exploring Grand Cayman in the Caribbean, where she lived and I was visiting, looking for non-touristy things to do. We'd heard about a subdivision that was built out of a mangrove swamp, then abandoned before it was finished. For reasons lost to time, we decided to take a look.

My sister drove her sedan into the development, going slowly along a road built through a forest of mangrove trees punctuated every so often by a house. We rolled up the windows and turned on the A/C because the humidity was increasing as we passed ditches and large drainage ponds. It was much darker than the bright day we'd left behind on the main road. We saw that some houses appeared occupied, but most were only partially built. The scene was a bit scary, and we made a joke about driving into a low-budget horror movie.

We noticed that the road had narrowed, and then unexpectedly we arrived at a dead end. We looked around and the only way to get out was to back up around a drainage pond. I should have gotten out and carefully guided my sister as she backed up and slowly swung the wheel. But I didn't, and Janie put the car in reverse.

Suddenly, we felt the back of the car give way. We were sliding down into the dark water of the pond! We couldn't see what was going on; we could only feel the pull of gravity. I yelled and Janie shrieked. The car hesitated and stopped. To my relief, no water got inside the car. I told Janie to put the car in park and slowly put on the handbrake—more to settle her nerves than any hope that those efforts would hold the car in place. She was crying, and her whole body was trembling. Ever since she was a baby, she'd not liked being in water and never wanted her head to be underwater. As a result, she was not a good swimmer.

The car was balanced precariously on the side of a steep bank. I had every expectation that we were going to keep sinking, but I didn't tell my sister. All she heard from me was a quiet voice asking her to do the next thing. Thinking we might slow the slide I said, "Let's very carefully open our doors and then push them with our legs as far as we can, to wedge them into the bank." I got my door wedged as far as possible into the steep bank and saw that it was very soft but hoped for some grip due to crisscrossed layers of reeds.

The car slid a bit more; Janie was terrified and cried, "Angie, Angie, we're going in! We're going in!"

That day I came to fully understand the term "having a death grip." Janie's fingers were wrapped around the steering wheel so tightly that all the blood had drained from them, and they were as pale as paper. Her right foot was pressed down so hard on the brake pedal that her leg quivered. How was I going to get her out before we slid further? I had to get around to her side of the car. I looked down and the water was a dark, murky brownish-black.

Janie knew I was a good swimmer and certified for scuba diving, so when I told her I was going to carefully slide into the water to come help her, she calmed a bit. Slowly and cautiously, I slid into the water and then promptly disappeared under the surface. As I went down, I did not feel a sloping bank or the pond bottom as I'd anticipated. There was only empty space. A growing dread gripped my heart. Janie shrieked as I popped up, reassuring her I was fine. I had to get her out as fast as possible because the pond was deeper than I thought. Quickly and gently, I used the car frame to guide myself around to her side. The car was sitting low enough that I could reach Janie without having to put any weight on the door frame.

First, I wedged her door more firmly into the bank and then explained each step we were going to take. I released her seatbelt and gradually convinced her to take her foot off the brake. In case the car slid, I had one hand on her left arm, ready to yank her out. She could not release her fingers, so I gently peeled them off one at a time saying, "Now the next one. Good. Now the next one."

When she had fully released the steering wheel, I explained that she had to slide into the water and I'd be right there to catch her. We'd go under the water, I said, but I would be able to get her head above the surface and then we'd float around the car door and climb up the bank. Finally, down she came, holding her breath as I asked, and we sank together briefly, then popped up to the surface. Still not feeling a bottom to the pond, I had a firm hold under her arms. We got away from the car and over to the slippery bank. The top layer of reeds came out of the soft soil as we tried to pull ourselves up with them, but with desperation as our fuel we clambered up and out.

What a moment! Safe! We'd expended what felt like gallons of adrenaline and our shaky bodies were soaking and covered in a film of slime. The pond water was brackish—a mix of salt and fresh water—and it stank. We looked like escapees from that horror movie we'd been joking about earlier as we sloshed along the road. This was years before cell phones, so we kept going to houses and knocking until we found someone with a landline willing to call the towing company.

Later, we learned that those drainage ponds were twenty to thirty feet deep. If we'd gone all the way in, we might never have been found. No one knew we were there that day. We were thankful to escape with just a bent drive shaft and a trunk full of brackish water.

In writing this story, I realized that life had given me something unexpected. We had actually escaped from a nightmare. Finally, I'd been able to rescue my sister.

In Loving Memory of Albert J.W. Hoy
December 7, 1928–December 9, 2024
You left this world speaking of love.

afterword

FOR SURVIVORS
Choosing the Path of Love

Forgiveness is giving up the idea that the past could have been any different, but we cannot move forward if we're still holding onto the pain of that past and wishing it was something else. OPRAH WINFREY[1]

This book about my childhood and life is for those who are living in the broken places, where the darkness is real and hope is scarce. Childhood abuse comes in many forms and can be profoundly debilitating. In addition, destructive family systems continue to damage adult survivors, often tearing away newfound normalcy. Healing is hard, incredibly hard, but help can come from unexpected places.

How does one begin to recover from a harmful family system? In my experience, the starting point was learning to understand what real love looks like.

Although my healing began when I chose the path of love, I saw that the route must travel over the mountain of forgiveness. I had to let go of bitterness, to uncover and grieve my losses and then break out of the shell of being a victim and live like a survivor—from the heart. I clung onto hope and gradually began my climb. It was a brutal journey. My sorrows had to be carefully unwrapped and given space, bucking years of conditioning from my mother who consistently laughed at and belittled my emotions, and from the men in her life who responded to my crying with cruelty. Slipping, sliding, scraping my heart, repeating and repeating heartbroken prayers, I pushed on and finally emerged out of an angry and restless state into a calm I'd never before known.

In her blog "The Corners," Nadia Bolz-Weber[2] talks about walking the Camino de Santiago and reaching Cruz de Ferro (the iron cross) at the top of a mountain, surrounded by a large field of stones. The stones had been carried many miles by pilgrims and were then piled at the foot of the cross. That location has become a physical depiction of the burdens people want to leave behind. Bolz-Weber says some of the rocks are quite large, others are small, and some have writing with "names and prayers and pleas for forgiveness." She says, "Both times I have stood at this sacred place I have wept." She prays "that none of us take it back." These images resonate with me. Forgiving truly means letting go of the weight, standing up, stretching, and looking at the horizon. Don't pick up the rock again. It's time to move on.

Being open and truthful about my feelings was, and still is, frightening. I sought counseling repeatedly; most of it helped. Just being heard without a violent or unkind response felt reassuring and validating. I spent time with friends who were supportive and caring and I threw off relationships that echoed the dysfunction of my childhood. (I also lost some precious friendships through my persistent dysfunction.) I gained strength with the understanding that forgiving those who had wronged me did not mean allowing predators or cruel people back into my life. These days I think of forgiving as a pardon to allow a fresh start.

I gave myself time to grieve, mourn, and lament those scared little girls and all they lost. I told myself that what happened to me as a child was not my fault. I forgave myself for the painfully bad choices of my young adult life and for the social dysfunction that infected my behavior right through my midlife.

FOR SURVIVORS WHO WANT TO RECOVER BUT WONDER IF THEY CAN

Don't give up. Despair will make its appearance, perhaps more often than you might expect, but refuse it a place to root. Guilt may plague you, but it's not yours. Anger will ransack your heart. You'll face your own awful mistakes. Courage will come, hope will follow, kind people will help you, and then you'll find one day that gratitude and maybe even delight will have arrived in your heart.

As author and podcaster Kate Bowler says, "You are not the bad thing." You are not forgotten, and you are loved. You deserve a good and peaceful life. Above all, your soul is beautiful and precious.

I invite you to consider asking God to give you strength to forgive and a path forward to a better life. Try to forgive him, too, if you are outraged that he didn't protect you. He is never far from any of us, and his love is endless. Look up and be amazed.

Jesus said, "Come to me, all you who are weary and burdened, and I will give you rest. Take my yoke upon you, and learn from me, for I am gentle and humble in heart, and you will find rest for your souls." (Matthew 11:28)

FOR MEMOIRISTS

There's somebody behind you. Someone who needs what you have, what you can offer. Who needs the peace that accompanies a new journey of

> hope. Not the stuff you have planned—your tidy package is nice, it looks good, but it's not the canvas God wants. It's that broken place, that place of shadows where miracles are born. Where the loveliness of your soul can burst forth and truly be seen. In the dark.   **TIFFANY BLUHM** [3]

Traveling back through the darkened corridors of a broken childhood is not for the faint of heart. I've read about memoirists who experienced sudden, serious illness, binge drinking, and other calamities that befell them as they wrote about their journeys.

I found to my surprise that I was no exception. Even though I'd sought counseling and done a tremendous amount of emotional work to recover, when I wrote this story and connected all of the pieces together, the completed account was startling and devastating. Up to that point, I had never seen my young life as an entire narrative, but rather as a series of disconnected, compartmentalized experiences. As I was editing my first full draft, I became seriously ill, depressed, and anxious. I experienced a complete personal upheaval and had to set aside the manuscript until my physical and mental health stabilized.

This memoir was driven by two pressing goals. It is meant to encourage other survivors to keep reaching for healing and truth. After a childhood filled with maltreatment, neglect, and deception, survivors need community and validation. In addition, this book identifies the enablers and abusers in my family lineage, which was corrupted by lies and denials crafted by my grandparents, my mother, and my non-related abusers. Names have been changed throughout this book to protect the living. Exposing truth can be a wild ride, but it's cleansing. Other distressing secrets can and often will emerge.

If you decide to write about childhood trauma, your road will be bumpy. Each person's experience is unique, but it will certainly be tough. I encourage you to get support and to be prepared for the unexpected. What you uncover may well hurt. Be kind to yourself and go only as fast as your heart can tolerate.

Above all, be a steadfast partner with the truth.

acknowledgments

An entire village of people have helped me write and publish my memoir.

Given the story arc of this book, I must begin by recognizing my living family. I give all of you my gratitude and love, especially for your support of and contributions to what has become our story. To my dear father and his sweet wife Marlene Parr: you have been a constant source of encouragement these past decades, and I cannot adequately articulate how much you have helped me heal. For my sister and brother-in-law Janie and Paul Cage: it's a continual delight to live life blessed by your love, friendship, and wit. To my wonderful husband Patrick, your steadfast love and your belief in my writing has nourished me. And I can't forget my cousin Adrienne, online sleuth and genealogy maven, who generously shared her lineage research and photos and patiently answered my late-night messages.

I am grateful to every friend who has cheered me on, answered questions about our shared history, read a draft, or offered to be a reader. Telling me you want to read this memoir is a balm for my uncertain writer's heart.

To kind and patient elementary and high school teachers everywhere: each of you is a treasure. Thank you for caring enough to stick with shy, weird, and difficult students; their transformation into confident adults is your greatest legacy. Furthermore, English literature and writing professors do not receive enough credit for their role in shaping writers. Since I earned my degree later in life, their impact is fresh in my mind. I salute Meg Roland, who is an unsinkable encourager and a fount of knowledge on female literary writers, and Perrin Kerns, who is an incredibly gracious critic and kept me going after our beloved university suddenly closed when I needed only five courses to graduate.

Two inspiring authors were kind enough to allow their words to be part of my story. I discovered David Tensen's poetry and podcasts during the pandemic; he is a true renaissance man from Down Under. Here in the Pacific Northwest, I've followed Tiffany Bluhm for some years and appreciate her vivacious spirit and powerful thinking.

This memoir would not exist without the vision and commitment of CEO Emily Barrosse, editor extraordinaire Karen Gulliver, and the entire team at Bold Story Press. You took a leaky boat and transformed it into a sleek sailing vessel. My hat is off to you.

endnotes

CHAPTER 2

1. The Imperial War Museum offers historical background on conscription in England during WW II and this civilian 'army.' What was the Women's Land Army in WW2? | Imperial War Museums (iwm.org.uk)

CHAPTER 7

1. See a map of Canada and the distances involved: Canada | History, Population, Immigration, Capital, & Currency | Britannica
2. Blitz bombings of English cities by Germany went on for nearly a year. Source: The Blitz Around Britain—World War 2 | Imperial War Museums (iwm.org.uk)
3. Axis nations at war against England and other allies were Germany, Italy, and Japan. Source and more information: Causes, events, and casualties of World War II | Britannica

CHAPTER 8

1. This site provides an overview of the vast size of the province and a map of its cities and towns: British Columbia | History, Facts, Map, & Flag | Britannica

CHAPTER 20

1. The Showboat stage still exists and offers summer entertainment: https://kitsilanoshowboat.com/

CHAPTER 25

1 David Tensen, *The Wrestle*: *Poems of Divine Disappointment and Discovery*, Saint Macrina Press, 2020, reprinted with permission. www.davidtensen.com

CHAPTER 37

1 As told by Paul Cage, my sister Janie's husband.

CHAPTER 38

1 From an unpublished memoir by Marlene Parr, wife of my father Albert Hoy. Because Marlene is only a few years older than me, she made me promise never to refer to her as my stepmother. I've kept that promise.

CHAPTER 46

1 Written by my sister Janie Cage.

AFTERWORD

1 Bruce D. Perry and Oprah Winfrey, *What Happened to You? Conversations on Trauma, Resilience, and Healing*, Flatiron Books, 2021. https://www.goodreads.com/quotes/10956201-forgiveness-is-giving-up-the-hope-that-the-past-could

2 Nadia Bolz-Weber "Cruz de Ferro," The Corners, June 4, 2024.

3 From "Where miracles are born," a message by Tiffany Bluhm, author of *Prey Tell* and *The Women We've Been Waiting For*. Used with permission. www.tiffanybluhm.com

about the author

Angela Hoy has always loved storytelling and books, which led to a career in communications and studies in English literature and writing. A graduate of Prescott College, she holds a bachelor's degree in arts and humanities, and is a member of Sigma Tau Delta, the International English Honor Society.

Never too far from the ocean, Angela lives and writes in the beautiful Pacific Northwest. She and her husband enjoy road trips and keep their passports ready for long-distance travel adventures. She shares her photos, poetry and more as @hoy.angela on Instagram and Threads. Find her blogs and stories at angelalhoy.substack.com.

about bold story press

Bold Story Press is a curated, woman-owned hybrid publishing company with a mission of publishing well-written stories by women. If your book is chosen for publication, our team of expert editors and designers will work with you to publish a professionally edited and designed book. Every woman has a story to tell. If you have written yours and want to explore publishing with Bold Story Press, contact us at https://boldstorypress.com.

The Bold Story Press logo, designed by Grace Arsenault, was inspired by the nom de plume, or pen name, a sad necessity at one time for female authors who wanted to publish. The woman's face hidden in the quill is the profile of Virginia Woolf, who, in addition to being an early feminist writer, founded and ran her own publishing company, Hogarth Press.

www.ingramcontent.com/pod-product-compliance
Lightning Source LLC
Chambersburg PA
CBHW032149080426
42735CB00008B/643